Covenant

and

Commandment

A STUDY OF THE TEN COMMANDMENTS
IN THE CONTEXT OF GRACE

By C. W. Christian

SMYTH&HELWYS
PUBLISHING, INCORPORATED · MACON, GEORGIA

To Elizabeth, Savannah, Sydney, and Eli

Smyth & Helwys Publishing, Inc.
6316 Peake Road
Macon, Georgia 31210-3960
1-800-747-3016
©2004 by Smyth & Helwys Publishing
All rights reserved.
Printed in the United States of America.

The paper used in this publication meets the minimum requirements of
American National Standard for Information Sciences—
Permanence of Paper for Printed Library Materials.
ANSI Z39.48–1984. (alk. paper)

Library of Congress Cataloging-in-Publication Data

Christian, C. W.
Covenant and commandment : a study of the Ten commandments in the context of grace
by C.W. Christian.
p. cm.
Rev. ed. of: The Ten commandments in the context of grace.
Includes bibliographical references.
ISBN 1-57312-426-5
1. Ten commandments-Criticism, interpretation, etc.
2. Covenants–Biblical teaching.
3. Grace–Biblical teaching.
I. Christian, C. W. Ten commandments in the context of grace
II. Title.
BS1285.52.C47 2004
222'.1606-dc21

2004000800

Contents

❦

Introduction: A Covenant with the Reader v

PART 1: The Covenant and the Commandments

Chapter 1: The God of Covenants...3

Chapter 2: The Hebrew Looks at God...13

Chapter 3: Humankind, Community, and History 29

Chapter 4: The Covenant and the Law 41

Chapter 5: The Ten Commandments:
       Their Origins, Character, and Scope 63

PART 2: The Vertical Commandments

Chapter 6: But First. . . A Word from God 83

Chapter 7: The First Commandment: 93
       The Character of God

Chapter 8: The Second Commandment: 101
       Concerning Idols

Chapter 9: The Third Commandment: 111
       On Using the Name

Chapter 10: The Fourth Commandment: 117
       Confessing Our Humanity

PART 3: The Horizontal Commandments

Chapter 11: "Let Persons Be Persons" 125

Chapter 12: The Fifth Commandment: 129
        Recognition of Indebtedness

Chapter 13: The Sixth Commandment: 137
        Respect for Persons as the Image of God

Chapter 14: The Seventh Commandment: 145
        Respect for Persons in the Male-Female Relationship

Chapter 15: The Eighth Commandment: 155
        Respect for Property as an Extension of Selfhood

Chapter 16: The Ninth Commandment: 165
        Respect for the Integrity of Society

Chapter 17: The Tenth Commandment:..171
        The Inwardness of the Law

Afterword: Down from the Mountain 175

Questions for Personal Reflection or Group Discussion 180

Introduction

❧

A Covenant with the Reader

WHAT KIND OF BOOK IS THIS?

Several years ago I purchased a book about the American Civil War from the sale table of a local bookseller. When some days later I began to read it, I quickly became frustrated. I lost patience with the careless scholarship of the historian and the numerous inaccuracies of detail. Characters of dubious historicity mingled with people named McLellan, Grant, Longstreet, Stuart, Stonewall Jackson, and Robert E. Lee. My frustration led me to look more closely at the credentials of the author, only to discover on the dust jacket three words I previously overlooked: "A Historical Novel." This was *fiction*! When I returned to the text—not a little abashed at my careless rush to judgment—I now found the unfolding narrative gripping, and persuasive.

In every meaningful or successful communication between the creator of the written word and the reader or consumer of that word there exists a covenant of discernment and understanding. It is the reader's part to deal honestly with the writer and with the writer's creation and to accurately discern the character of the text, including the intentions and purposes of the writer. It is the reader's part to avoid forcing purposes and intentions on the text that are foreign to the writer's purposes. Failing to do so is courting misunderstanding.

Not all truth is expressed in the same way. The truth of a novel is not the truth of a history textbook, nor do we search for the meaning of a poem in the same way that we ask about the meaning of a philosophical proposition or an essay on physics. Different genres "speak" in different ways and must be read according to their speaking.

What is the writer's part in this covenant of understanding? Is it not to communicate that vision cogently to the reader? Therefore, part of the writer's duty is to make clear to himself and to his potential readership what audience he seeks to address, so that the reader may determine whether to invest time and energy in reading the work.

To whom is this book addressed? It is intended not for the professional biblical or scholarly community—although I would hope it has sufficient integrity of scholarship to merit the approval of that community. It is intended rather for the intelligent and inquiring layperson or minister, and especially for the layperson who is not sure that the Bible as a whole is significant for responsible modern living and who may be even less sure about the relevance of the Old Testament.

I also hope it might find among its readers the kind of audience that has played a key role in shaping the book's insights. It reflects the influence of several generations of college students whose curiosity about the Bible and about Christian theology has provided me with continuing stimulation and challenge. I have been impressed by the seriousness with which many college and university students take both the biblical heritage and the responsibility to understand it and live it.

In short, this book is directed to intelligent, thinking, and inquiring Christians who would like to consider how their faith relates to and participates in the rich but sometimes opaque heritage in the Hebrew Scriptures. I will attempt to speak to the thoughtful person who has felt uncomfortable with the easy and shallow application of biblical dicta to the complex social, ethical, and political issues of the present but who by instinct, heritage, or conviction is prepared to take the biblical faith seriously and find it relevant to life in the world.

BOOTLEGGING THEOLOGY

When asked to speak to religious groups, Dr. Abner McCall, former president of Baylor University and a widely respected layman, always made it clear that he did not carry papers of ordination. Rather, he said, he was "a bootlegger of the gospel." There is a sense in which this volume aims at more than the title might suggest, and to keep my covenant of honesty with the reader, I must make this *more* plain.

It is, indeed, a biblical study, an examination of the traditions and texts of the Hebrews. Its insights and interpretations were developed through forty years of teaching the Old Testament to more than 10,000 college students. But its perspectives on the Old Testament have been shaped and colored by my primary training and commitment. I am a theologian by trade. This needs to be understood in case I am suspected of bootlegging Christian theology into the Old Testament. Far from denying such a charge, I confess it gladly! Still, widespread misunderstanding about the theologian's task and theology's place in biblical and church life makes brief explanations necessary.

Although there have been obscure and abstruse *theologies*, there is nothing abstruse or mysterious about theology. Theology is what happens when we reflect on our experience of God and of life in the world. It is the verbal expression (whether spoken or thought) of religious experience. Theology is our thought about God and about all our insights and encounters that have anything to say about God. It is our attempt to give expression—as consistently and accurately as possible—to insights that in some respects lie too deep for words. Theology is what we think and say about our faith and about God.

If this is a valid definition of theology, it becomes clear that every person who has ever given thought to faith, however primitive and imperfect, is a theologian. The believer has no option about being a theologian. The only available choice is between a thoughtful, consistent, and creative theology and a fragmentary, confused, or uncreative one.

EXPLANATORY DOCTRINES

We have argued that theology is our attempt to express our religious experiences in words. But our words at their best carry the imperfections of language in general and our own language in particular. This means that no doctrinal expression, either of an individual or a church, can express the truth of God fully and without flaw. All theology is in the final analysis human. Every doctrine is an attempt to find words adequate to the reality we have met. Thus we must always be ready to "listen through" religious language and expression in order to hear the underlying reality and truth. Difficult theological notions often become clearer and more meaningful if we can trace them back to the experiences they seek to explain. I call these "explanatory doctrines." There will be occasions in the following pages when this phrase will be helpful in clarifying our meaning.

It is also clear that any biblical study is inescapably a theological study. If theology is our reflection on God and our experience of God, then the whole text of Scripture takes on a theological cast, since it consists of the confessions of men and women who lived and expressed the life of faith. We will ask how the Hebrews understood the world, themselves, and God in the wake of their great encounter in the exodus. But since their experience and their reflection has become part of the Christian story, we will not hesitate to see them in the light of the Christian faith and tradition.

Since this book is primarily a theological interpretation of a well-known part of the Old Testament, it is not intended for devotional reading, even though we will be concerned with the practical implications of law and covenant. Nor, as we have said, should it be seen as a careful exegetic or textual analysis, although I will not hesitate to avail myself of the work of such scholarship.

It is also not intended to be read without serious effort. I hope it is in no way difficult or unapproachable. Nevertheless, I will not hesitate to ask the reader to wrestle with ideas that will carry him or her beyond the devotional level, but that may have the power to open up new dimensions of meaning in the Decalogue and in the Hebrew and Christian traditions. Some passages may require rereading and careful digestion, especially when they ask the reader to rethink old ideas in different ways.

The language used may also from time to time ask for close attention. I will seek to avoid the scholar's tone, but I will not hesitate to ask the reader to engage new or unfamiliar words, especially where such words will help clarify and deepen our insight into the text.

My inescapable focus will be the faith tradition in which I exist. As I have suggested above, I will not hesitate to interpret covenant and law through Christian eyes, and this is a confession that will be looked upon in some scholarly circles as unworthy. In fact, for some it will disqualify the whole project. There are certainly good reasons for caution in the approach we will take, and there is undeniably more in the Hebrew Scriptures than is likely to be discerned through the perspective of Christian faith. But it is still a legitimate enterprise. This is and will remain the case so long as the Christian community accepts the Old Testament as a part of its sacred Scriptures. By claiming for themselves the Hebrew Scriptures, Christians affirm that the roots of their own distinctive understanding of God, humankind, and the world are still deep in those ancient writings.

Martin Luther's "Christocentric" principle for the interpretation of the Old Testament—namely, that we find its authority for faith in its foreshadowing of Christ—is decisive if Christians are to acknowledge the Old Testament as part of their sacred canon. However, such a procedure is risky. Often this "viewing through Christ" has resulted in the distortion of what Luther himself called the "plain historical meaning" of the Old Testament. It has led to sometimes fantastic speculations and to the "discovery" of "typologies" of Christ and of Christian doctrine everywhere in its pages, often where a clear, unprejudiced eye could see that none existed. Nevertheless, it is still true that the Old Testament remains normative for Christians only because it speaks meaningfully to the faith that is the heart of the Christian story.

While the Christian would not be a Christian without assuming the embracing character of the New Testament vision, the continuity of the Hebrew and Christian visions has been affirmed throughout Christian history. Again, Christians affirm this unity when they call the Hebrew canon *Scripture*. Although the two faiths are not identical, in most respects they stand on the same ground, or, to use a more contemporary metaphor, they share the same horizon. The question then becomes, "How does the Hebrew vision illuminate the Christian vision?"

STORY AND HISTORY

What we have said above means that we acknowledge the Judeo-Christian community as our chief context, and this provides the frame of reference for this book. This frame of reference will guide us in the selection of themes and materials and also in their interpretation and application. The following study will be an interpretation based on the "story" of a community in which we assume both the writer and the reader will participate. To the extent that Jews and Christians share a common heritage, it will be "our" shared story. We will seek to set the commandments within a narrative framework. We will not ask, at least at the beginning, about the objective "truth" of that story or the universal applicability of the life-principles or laws it sets forth for living.

By asking about the meaning of law and covenant within the framework of *story*, we will recognize several things. First, we will acknowledge the narrative character of the Hebrew mind and therefore of the Hebrew Scriptures. Occasionally a student in one of my Old Testament introductory courses will comment that mostly what we do in class is "tell stories." I usually congratulate such a student for discovering a fundamental fact about what it was to be a

Hebrew and about how the Hebrew looked at the world. Story is the Hebrew vehicle for truth. This fact is reflected in the structure of the Hebrew language, which is largely built upon verbs and tends to center meaning in *events*, rather than in objects. This fact is not unrelated to the Hebrew manner of conceiving God and God's relationship to the world. If you ask a Greek to explain the nature of things, he will offer you a logical syllogism or draw for you a diagram. If you ask a Hebrew the same question, he will tell you a story.

Second, when we inquire about the meaning of covenant and law as a part of the Hebrew/Christian story, we acknowledge the current widespread interest in narrative as a vehicle for meaning. Experts in many of the scholarly disciplines—literature, philosophy, sociology, and psychology among them—have in the last few decades become aware that in all human society the story is the basic means of communicating moral, communal, and theological meaning. In this sense, we will be doing a kind of narrative biblical theology. This narrative nature of our enterprise will determine the kinds of questions we bring to the text. It will also mean that some kinds of questions often asked of the Hebrew Scriptures will have secondary or even marginal interest for us.

For instance, we will not be greatly interested in the historical or archeological accuracy of the Hebrew story. Indeed, we will assume that Israel's own telling of its story, however ancient her memories, were codified and given their definitive shape well after the exodus. We will not become embroiled in the question whether the exodus and conquest and settlement narrative as recorded in the Hexateuch—the first six books of the Old Testament—are consistent with the archeological record as now interpreted. We won't worry about whether the process of nation-forming described in Judges and in the Samuel literature can be accepted as historical. These questions, interesting and important as they are, are not the sort we ask of the storyteller.

Several years ago I counseled a student who was having personal problems. In one session, the student confided to me a childhood experience of great terror that, she reported, still reappeared in her dreams. Later, in conversation with the student's parents, I found that the episode was actually so different from what she had told me that it was hardly the same event.

What would have been the proper response to the student when she approached me afterward? Should I discard her account as meaningless and dismiss her as unworthy of my future trust and confidence? Had she not badly misled me? Or would such behavior on my part have been irresponsible in the extreme, because as a counselor and friend I was not primarily concerned with the facts? I did not care about what some might call "external history." Nor did I care about the accuracy of her recollection. I was much more concerned with *personal* history, with what those facts, having passed into the flux of her life, came to mean to *her*, the person who had lived them.

Now, while the Hebrew story is rich with the raw materials for historical inquiry and reconstruction, it is nonetheless *their* story. It is not "mere history," in the sense of a bare recitation of facts, but *interpreted* history. It is events recorded and shaped by the Hebrews' need to understand for themselves and to tell to subsequent generations who they were, how they got that way, and where they hoped to go. Thus it is no surprise that their remembrance of past things was shaped and altered by subsequent history. The Hebrews did not hesitate to retell their story and to alter it in light of subsequent experiences, just as each of us lives, relives, retells, and reunderstands the pivotal events of our respective lives. This Hebrew reliving and reunderstanding is witnessed to by the frequency in the Old Testament of "twice-told tales," in which the specifics of the tellings are significantly different. It is witnessed to by the manner in which pre-exodus history is reshaped and given meaning by the unforgettable events of the exodus itself.

Such a distinction between personal history and external history will be troubling to some, since in each case we are confronting the phenomenon of time and asking about the meaning of events. Can a story be true and important in any sense if it is not true in every sense? Can the *meaning* of a story be distinguished from its *facts*? It isn't rare for students who become aware for the first time of the many historical problems posed by the Hebrew Scriptures to dismiss the Old Testament in its entirety. My attempt to distinguish between the meaning of the story and the details of its telling is sometimes lost on them. "If I can't believe all of it," they tell me, "then I can't believe any of it." Yet the same students make different demands upon their own stories or the stories of friends or of their generation.

ON SELECTING OUR PAST

Our concern, then, will be to unfold the story of the Hebrews as it ordered and shaped their awareness of being a people, and to understand, at least in some limited respects, how it has been incorporated into and illuminated by the story of the church.

Every story is selective. As we tell our story we highlight events and encounters that throw light on who we are and how we got that way. In fact, every story has its central event or constellation of events in the light of which the past is re-remembered and newly understood and in the light of which the future is dreamed of, planned for, and acted upon. Now, to attempt to tell *our* story—meaning the shared story of Hebrew and Christian—and to do so from the special point of reference of the Christian community is to admit to selectivity. In the present study, we will have three main points of focus:

(1) We will focus our attention on the event that was for the Hebrews absolutely central: the exodus. (2) We will consider what its implications were for the central event of the Christian story: that of Christ. The fact that the Christian faith can embrace the exodus as its own is a measure of how deeply the two stories are bound together.

There are most certainly other, sometimes contrary, themes and motifs in the richness of the Old Testament than those of exodus, covenant, and Decalogue on which we will concentrate. Likewise, there are elements in the Christian experience that remind us that the two faiths are not always and at every point compatible. We will argue that no Hebrew/Christian story is possible that ignores these pivotal realities.

(3) We will also ask about the relevance of that story to the larger story of humankind. Our selectivity in handling the Hebrew story will not reflect merely its exodus experience and Christ event. It will reflect our situation in the late twentieth and early twenty-first century. Because we live in a different epoch, we may ask of our Hebrew predecessors questions that they in their own time might not have dreamed of. We will attempt to assess the relevance of the Hebrew notion of covenant and of the Ten Commandments for life in our world. The infinite variety of problems that confronts the believer in our day—for instance, questions of genetic engineering, organ transplants, prenatal sex determination, environmental preservation, or nuclear warfare—reveal the impossibility of a simplistic biblicism.

If biblical faith is relevant to our world, it must be able to speak to questions such as these. Our concern will be to ask whether the Hebrew vision, as understood through the embracing perspective of the Christian vision, can speak meaningfully to our world. In other words, we must ask at a later point in our study whether there is a connection between our story and "the" Story.

NOTES

[1] Henri Bergson, *Creative Evolution*, trans. Arthur Mitchell (New York: The Modern Library, Random House, 1944), 11f.

[2] Sam Keen, *To a Dancing God: Notes of a Spiritual Traveler* (New York: Harper Collins Publishers, 1970, 1990), 25.

Part One

~

The Covenant and the Commandments

Chapter One

∽

The God of Covenants

TESTAMENT AND COVENANT

The sacred Scriptures of the Christian community are divided into two collections of writings commonly called the Old and New Testaments. Many years ago when I was serving a church as interim pastor, I was asked to lead a group of adults in studying a selected book of the Bible. When I asked the group what particular book of the Bible they would like to study, I did not get a ready response, so I prompted them further: "Would you like to study an Old Testament book or a New Testament book?" Again I received no response. Finally, an elderly woman spoke: "Could I ask a question?" This was a woman who had been teaching an adult Sunday school class for more than thirty years and was well-versed in Scripture. "This may sound silly," she continued, "but what is a testament?"

What is a testament? Why do we refer to the Hebrew Scriptures and the specifically Christian Scriptures as testaments? The word is not commonly used in English except in reference to the Bible. It is clearly akin to such words as "testify" and "testimony," as all three derive from a common Latin root, *testate*, to bear witness.

Like both *testify* and *testimony*, the word *testament* has legal ramifications. In fact, its only other common English use is in the setting of court and legal chamber. At one point in my life, I began to consider my own mortality and concluded that I needed to take steps to prepare for the eventuality of death. I had concerns about my family and also about my modest property—which my attorney insisted on referring to, rather grandly, as my "estate." Accordingly, he drew up and executed for me a "Last Will and Testament." A testament, in legal terminology, is what we commonly call a will, and as such it is a legal document. The word *testament* is in fact a direct rendering into English of the Latin word for a will, *testimentum*. A testament is a will.

What is the purpose of a will? Why does one bother to execute such a document? I made my will in the hope that I might be able to exercise some measure of control over the direction of my affairs when I am no longer present to oversee them. Legally a will is a contract of sorts, and like all contracts it involves a binding commitment between two or more parties. Who are the parties to the contract that we call a will or testament? The testator or maker of the will? The legatees or beneficiaries? All of these, to be sure! But who else? In actual fact, every member of the society is effectively involved in the agreement that constitutes a will. That is what we mean when we call it a *legal* document. A will is a contract between the testator and the whole of the society, in which the members of that society promise to abide by the wishes and the intentions of the will maker when the will is activated by his or her death.

As with all contracts, the primary reason for making a will is the reassurance of the parties of the will. I enter into contracts, whether legal or personal, in order to create with the contractual partner a situation or a relationship on which I can rely. Indeed, in a legal contract I have the force of compulsion to regulate the conduct of my partners so as to assure that they will not nullify or transgress their commitments to me.

When we move from the legal sphere to the sphere of personal relationships, a word like "contract" may sound inappropriately sterile or forbidding. If I enter into a deeply personal relationship with another human being involving affection and commitment, I am apt to employ different language. Witness the most intimate of human relations: In Anglo-Saxon tradition, it is not common to speak of a marriage *contract* but, perhaps more commonly, of a marriage *covenant?* When five decades ago I stood by the side of a young woman and we spoke to one another words of promise, we entered a covenant of marriage.

I propose that we consider carefully the implications of the notion of covenant, for with it we confront the word that more than any will dominate our study. A testament is a covenant, and despite habit it would be well if the

Christian community could come to refer to the two major scriptural divisions as the Old Covenant and the New Covenant.

"I ESTABLISH MY COVENANT WITH YOU"

Some years ago I received as a gift a beautiful, leather-bound Bible, a special edition prepared by a Christian group that made much of its superior understanding a Scripture. It was a handsome book and I often used it in classroom and pulpit. One day I consulted this Bible while preparing a lecture. I wanted to refer to a text with which I was familiar but the exact reference for which I could not recall. I turned to the back of the Bible to consult the combination Bible concordance and dictionary it contained.

As many of my readers will know, a biblical concordance is a reference tool that catalogues alphabetically the key words in the Bible along with Scripture phrases and references in which the word occurs. The passage I sought contained the word "covenant." To my astonishment, this concordance did not even include the word. My curiosity aroused, I estimated the number of words catalogued in the concordance to be about 1,500. It included figs, doorposts, harlots, and heifers, but no covenant! Yet this omission is symptomatic of the absence of a critical and formative theme in pulpit and classroom. Many readers of these words will have spent much of their lives in a church pew without hearing a sermon on the theme of covenant.

Throughout the Bible, God is described as a God who makes covenants. There is perhaps no more persistent or more fruitful metaphor for understanding both the Hebrew and the Christian faith than this one. Both Hebrew and Christian Scriptures are saturated by the theme of divine covenant-making. In the Hebrew Scriptures, God could be said to have established an implicit covenant in the act of creation, but with the conclusion of the great flood narrative the theme of covenant-making becomes explicit. God "establishes" his covenant, not only with Noah and his sons and through them with their seed, but with all the creatures of the earth as well (Gen 9).

The Hebrews' own story begins with covenant-making, as God enters into covenant with Abraham. The whole of the patriarchal saga of Abraham and his sons and grandsons is the struggle of the Hebrew founder to comprehend, realize, and transmit Yahweh's covenant with him and his people. And if the covenant with Abraham means birth as a people, the Sinai saga, centering on the figure of Moses, means rebirth as a covenant nation.

The story of Israel after Sinai is told, especially in the Deuteronomic history, as a struggle to understand and preserve the sense of covenant and the mission it entailed against the corrupting influence of nation and power. When that struggle seemed to fail, the great prophetic tradition arose to rescue the covenant from disaster and then, with Jeremiah, to proclaim the coming of a *New* Covenant. The Christian community revealed its continuity with the Hebrew covenant faith and the God of covenants by declaring that Jeremiah's proclamation had become a reality. If the Hebrews understood themselves as people of the covenant, the Christians saw themselves as people of the "New Covenant."

It is no historical accident that the picture of God as covenant-maker so dominates the biblical tradition. It is an attempt to say something fundamental about the character of God. And the character of God is itself fundamental to everything else in life. What God is like matters! Then what is the Hebrew trying to say when he describes God as a covenant-maker?

Covenant as Assurance

We suggested above that the central purpose of covenant-making is the reassurance of the covenantal partner or partners. Therefore a critical element of every contract or covenant is *self-limitation.* That is what it means to speak of such covenants as commitments and to call them "binding." One who is bound, be it human or God, is no longer in every respect free. This is true whether the contract is legal and subject to enforcement by coercion, or personal and dependent on the good will and moral consistency of the partners. In the act of promise I guarantee to my covenant partner a certain specificity of conduct! I will do certain things; others I will refrain from doing. Thus the covenant fellow or partner can live out of the reliability of my promise. So it is that the first explicit example of divine promise-making in Scripture—the promise made to Noah after the flood—has at its heart a self-limitation. God says to Noah, "I establish my covenant with you that never again will all flesh be cut by the waters of a flood" (Gen 8:11).

The positive strength of every meaningful covenant lies in its exclusions—in its self-limitations. I employed above the example of my own marriage covenant. At the end of that solemn ceremony, with our vows fully spoken, my new bride and I strode up the aisle and through the church door. As we passed through its portals I reached into my pocket and tossed into the bushes—not literally, but metaphorically—my "little black book." The meaning of the vows that I had just taken was "to you only"! I had asked this woman to separate herself from father and mother, and the only reassurance I could give her for making this bold divorcement was in the certainty that my commitment was complete, and that she could bank on it. That meant that in subsequent years when I called to report to her that I would be working late at the office, she could be sure I was working late at the office. "For better, for worse, for richer, for poorer, in sickness and health, 'til death do us part!" The integrity of her hopes and her future depended on the integrity of my promise.

Thus when the Hebrew described God as a covenant-maker, he was quick to point out the divine self-limitation. Because God enters into covenants, he can be trusted. And if *God* can be trusted, then *life* in the world can be trusted. The deep positivism and final optimism of biblical religion is rooted in this sense of the divine self-limitation. This deep confidence in the trustworthiness of God allowed the Hebrew to see the whole of creation as "good" and always—even after the fall—as redeemable. Perhaps we can reduce this sense of the divine reliability to a memorable formula: *God is the kind of God who makes promises and keeps them.*

This theme of the promise-keeping God lies at the heart of the great exodus narrative from its beginning. Thus at the episode of the burning bush in Exodus 3 and 4, God describes himself not as a new and unknown God introducing himself to Moses and the people of Israel but rather as the God of Abraham, Isaac, and Jacob. Promises were made to these men and to their children, promises that Yahweh was even then in Egypt about to fulfill. The exodus is God's act of faithfulness to his promised word.

Covenant as Community Forming

The Hebrew story, despite its focus upon figures depicted in heroic terms, is nevertheless the story of community. The great moments of covenant-making are set in the context of God's dealing with individuals—Noah, Abraham, Jacob, Moses, David—but in every case his binding of himself to such and such an individual sets forth and creates a larger community for which the hero stands. The Noachic covenant, which first of all embraces Noah and his immediate family, embraces also through them the larger human community depicted in its lineal descent from Noah's sons. And the promise given is the basis for a community even more embracing, for it binds together both man and nature.

The covenant with Abram/Abraham depicts the creation of a special covenant of God with the man himself, but it also announces the birth of a people who will live out of that continuing fellowship. Abraham will become a great nation. Furthermore, it anticipates a widening community in which, by invoking Abram's name, "all the families of the earth will bless themselves" (Gen 12:3). If the Abraham covenant describes the birth of the tribal community, then the covenant at Sinai is the birth of the nation proper by the gracious act of God. This means that the Hebrew law and its classic expression in the Ten Commandments are not fully comprehensible apart from the community of grace that is its expression.

Covenant as Grace

The practice of covenant-making by no means originated with the Hebrews. Indeed, it already had a lengthy history before Moses. In fact, recent archeological discoveries in the fertile crescent have provided evidence of a significant number of international covenants as well as of covenental agreements between sovereigns and people,[1] some of which have striking parallels with the covenant formulas of Israel. Some of these documents can be dated to the third millennium BC and thus at least 1,500 years prior to usual dates assigned to the exodus. Examples have been found in ancient Chaldea, Mesopotamia, and among the royal Hittite archives in what today is Turkey.

Two basic types of such ancient covenants are usually identified, (1) the *parity* covenant, where the contracting parties stand on the same level and deal on equal terms, and (2) the *suzerainty* covenant, where the establishment of the covenant or agreement is unilateral—that is, where one of superior status, such as a lord or emperor, establishes the covenant and bestows it on the recipients. The parity covenant is essentially an international kind of contract, since only reigning princes were likely to be in position to participate in the necessary negotiations. Sarna describes such a covenant that was concluded between Hattusilis III, king of the Hittites, and Rameses II of Egypt. This great contract, which ended a long and bloody rivalry, was executed at about the time of the Hebrew exodus.

Given the nature of the political and imperial power in the ancient Near East, the suzerainty covenant is the most common. Whether such a contract is addressed by a conqueror to a subject people or by a lord to his own people, the initiative for the covenant lies with the sovereign.

It is likely that the Hebrew notion of *b'rit* or covenant was influenced by more ancient models, especially the Hittite suzerainty covenants. Such covenants commonly show a more or less clear formula. Sarna describes the elements of such covenant formulations:

First comes the preamble in which the initiator of the treaty is identified by name, and his titles, attributes, and genealogy are listed. Next comes a historical review in which the past relationships of the contracting parties are set forth. In particular . . . there is a reminder of the previous benefactions bestowed by the suzerain upon the vassal . . . then follow the *stipulations*, which are the core of the treaty; the call for the deposition of the document in the vassal's sanctuary . . . and finally, a statement of curses and blessings.[2]

The question of how closely the Hebrew covenant and especially the Sinai covenant pattern follow this ancient model will be examined later. The point of importance at this stage of our discussion is to dispel a common misunderstanding regarding the religious meaning of covenant in the Old Testament. In general, the Hebrew understood that the covenants of God with his people were by no means parity covenants. Even where the covenant was seen to be dependent on the sustained faithfulness of Israel, *its origin was with God.* To be sure, they were not above the kind of legalistic understanding that converted God's dealings into a mutuality contract, but when they were thinking at their best they understood that not only the origin of covenant lay in the hands of God but also its *continuity* and *survival.*

It is of considerable importance that the preceding sentence be taken seriously, because it provides us with a healthy corrective to a common misunderstanding of the relation of law and covenant in biblical tradition. It is sometimes maintained that God established the covenant but that its success and perseverance, and especially the continued participation of a nation or an individual in it, is determined by covenant performance, as codified in covenant law. That is, whether or not a people or an individual would remain a part of God's family was to be determined by their obedience.

It is certainly true that Israel struggled with this issue: namely, the relationship between covenant obedience and divine grace—a matter we will examine carefully in a later chapter. But as Israel tells her own story, the sheer existence of the people of the covenant springs from an act of grace. This is the source of the sense of awe that often hovers around the covenant confessions of the Old Testament. The notion of election, whether in the Mosaic writings or in Paul's letter to the Ephesians, always combines a sense of assurance and amazement.

The popular resentment often expressed against the notion of a "chosen people" arises from failure to grasp this sense of astonishment. It is often assumed that the election of Israel arose from Israel's superior virtue or worth, that Israel is to be seen as "better" than her neighbors and so worthy of the divine favor. But it is clear that this is not the way the Hebrew understood it, except when his understanding was degraded into the easy and self-serving legalism to which every religion can fall victim. There was no sense of greater deserving or superior worth. When the Hebrews faced the reality of their calling, what they seemed to find was an impenetrable mystery. At their most clear-headed, they were overwhelmed by their unworthiness for the divine friendship.

The great confession in Deuteronomy 26 makes clear this sense of awe at the divine act of including them. "Who were we to be so favored?" they seem to ask. "Where was our superior worth or potential?" After all, Moses confessed on behalf of each Hebrew,

> A wandering Aramean was my ancestor; he went down into Egypt and lived there as an alien, few in number, and there he became a great nation, mighty and populous. When the Egyptians treated us harshly and afflicted us . . . the LORD brought us out of Egypt with a mighty hand. (Deut 26:5-8)

This confession fairly crackles with a sense of the divine mystery, goodness, and trustworthiness. The covenant rested in its inception on nothing more than the divine good favor, on *grace*! And its persistence and survival rested just as surely on God's *sustaining* grace. The divine creativity of the world was never thought of as initiatory only but as sustaining; so also the covenant is dependent on God's continuing faithfulness to his promise in every moment.

A recurrent theme in God's dealing with Abraham and his sons is the futility of depending on Israel's loyalty or faithfulness or of relying on her strength of character to sustain her fellowship with him. The patriarchal narratives beginning in Genesis 12 rarely commend the fathers for their virtue, reliability, or worth. Far from being examples of faith, they are more often depicted as men of little vision and as profoundly unworthy of God's special care. The writer confronts us repeatedly with a sharp contrast between the faithlessness of the patriarchs and the faithfulness of God. Abraham, having received the promise of a great nation, agonized over God's tardiness in providing for the fulfillment of that promise, even rebuking God to his face.

This gulf between the promise of a son and the nonfullfillment of that promise provides the dramatic tension for the Abraham saga. In Genesis 15, God is depicted as confronting the patriarch with reassuring words and with promises of blessing, only to receive the stinging rebuke of a frustrated patriarch: "What can you give me, seeing I remain childless!" Undeterred by

Abraham's unworthy response, God calmly repeats and deepens his promise, binding the patriarch to him by both word and act.

The account of covenant renewal in Genesis 15 is followed in the next chapter by a delightful human drama. Its witty portrayal of the three principles in the arrangement that led to the birth of Ishmael—the taunting revenge of Hagar, raised to a new status by her pregnancy, the jealous projection of Sarah's anger onto the husband, and Abraham's neat husbandly sidestepping of responsibility—may obscure the sly commentary on the unworthiness of Abraham and his clan. In the shadow of the great renewal in Genesis 15, Abraham and Sarah, distrustful of God's competence or reliability, try to run ahead of the divine fulfillment and establish the covenant on their own. But despite their flagging trust, God goes quietly forward toward the fulfillment of his promises.

Even the great climactic covenant renewal described in Genesis 17 reasserts, with wonderfully ironic humor, that the covenant rests not on worth or on the rock-bound faith of the recipient but on grace. Again it is God who initiates and formalizes his covenant relation with Abraham. In the initial exchange between divine covenant-maker and patriarch, Abram, now to become Abraham, is described as "falling on his face"—in reverence and adoration?—before God! When God shocks him with the announcement that his aged wife is about to bear a son, Abraham falls on his face again, not in reverence but in a helpless heap of laughter. The "giant of faith," overcome by the ridiculousness of the promise, presses on his covenant partner the need for practicality in such matters. He pleads with God, "O that Ishmael might live in thy sight."

Even God's response to this signal failure of faith is not without its ironic humor, for the child born to Sarah will be called "Isaac," which means "he laughs." By the bestowing of this whimsical name, it is guaranteed that the patriarch will never address his son without being reminded of how he responded to the divine promise. It is not a matter of faith but *faithfulness*—the faithfulness of God, that is—that sustains the promise.

The contrast of patriarchal faithlessness and divine faithfulness informs the Jacob cycle as well. The selection of the devious Jacob rather than the open-handed Esau has embarrassed teachers of children for generations. I recall my childhood Sunday school teacher explaining that Jacob was chosen because he was really the better man since he understood the value of the birthright and blessing. The Hebrew saga makes no such point. Jacob was a rascal! Nor did his theft of the blessing constitute his selection as the covenant son. That selection came to him by divine revelation at Bethel and it rested on nothing more fundamental than the divine good will! And the very "deal" that he announced in response to this awesome encounter—that if God would do him good he would give God a tithe of his riches—is a sly commentary on his unworthiness. This naive expression of what we will call legalism has been described as the "nursery floor" of religion. Indeed, throughout the Jacob story the survival of covenant depends not on the faith of Jacob but on God. He is preserver, sustainer, and renewer.

In slightly altered form the theme persists in the final patriarchal cycle dealing with Joseph. Here the contrast between faith and unfaith is between Joseph and his faithless covenant brothers, whose nefarious plot offers to destroy the covenant hopes centered in Rachel's son. But what his brothers intended for evil God makes to work out for good, as Joseph's banishment to Egypt becomes the prelude to the exodus.

The patriarchal narratives, in their stress on the covenant as divine good favor in action, lay the foundation for a powerful tension and conflict. What bearing can the divine goodwill toward Israel have on the question of the divine good favor toward the rest of humanity? Even if the covenant with Abraham and his children rested on no special merit on their part, yet they were to be God's people. The initial announcement of the promise to Abram (Gen 12:1-3) is replete with the language of privilege and exclusiveness, and yet the cryptic concluding provision seems to set privilege in the context of duty. It is twice stated: ". . . so that you will *be* a blessing," and "in thee and thy seed shall all families of the earth bless themselves." More will be said about the tension between particularism and universalism in Israel's faith.

NOTES

[1] Nahum Sarna, *Exploring Exodus: The Heritage of Biblical Faith* (Napierville IL: Alec R. Allenson, Inc., 1965), 134-36.

[2] Ibid.

~

Chapter Two

The Hebrew
Looks at God

How one looks upon or thinks about God profoundly shapes one's perspectives on everything else. I suggest this is the case regardless of the nature of that thinking. If by the word "God" we can understand "whatever is fundamental to all reality and experience," then the proposition becomes a truism. How you view ultimate reality tends to shape your sense of value and priority, your ethics, your expectations and hopes. One who believes in a "cruel god," like Verdi's Iago, is not likely to see the world as a benign place or behave toward his neighbors with charity and forbearance. And the rejection of any notion of God, as in theoretical atheism, is never without its ramifications in the larger areas of ethics and human endeavor.

The Hebrews were in most regards, at least in the beginning, people of their time and of their world. The day is past when we can artificially separate the religion and life of the Hebrews from the cultural and religious currents of their culture. The more we come to know about that world, the clearer we can see how much of it the Hebrews shared. In most respects they were much like their neighbors. Yet even from those early centuries in which their self-understanding took shape there were differences.

For instance, while their debt to the older covenant models of the Hittites are striking, the notion of covenant in Israelite faith is not a repetition of the older pattern. It is touched, as we will see below, by a special Hebrew genius that roots in a fundamental vision of God.

I propose that despite the many levels and the complexity of Hebrew faith, there are certain basic elements in the way the Israelite saw the world and the place of humankind in it. I am also suggesting that the view of God that undergirded the Hebrew worldview functioned like leaven to render Hebrew tradition increasingly distinct with the passing centuries. These differences become clear as the Hebrew tells his story. At bottom much of the difference was related to certain more-or-less distinctive notions about God.

How did this distinctive view arise? The Hebrews would answer, "It arose from our encounter with God." The Hebrew story is one of confrontation with God. Where and when had they met God? While they came to understand theirs as a whole history lived in the divine presence, the great decisive event appears to have been that which we call the exodus. There can be little doubt that for the Hebrew the transforming experience in their history was this great and unforgettable episode. As they understood it, God had, by a mighty hand, reached into the lives of a people headed for obscurity, if not total assimilation, to give them a sense of purpose and destiny. The exodus is the pivotal event in the light of which they reunderstood and reinterpreted everything else in their history. In the light of the exodus, they came to understand the patriarchal traditions as the prevenient act of the God whose final outworking was their deliverance from Egypt.

What was this Hebrew God like? I suggest that from these earliest beginnings, certain fundamental ways of conceiving God informed Israel's whole history as a people. I need to speak a word of caution about the way in which I will set forth that vision of God, for I will use the language and the forms of late Hebrew prophetism. Indeed, I could be accused of filching my categories almost without modification from the thought of the great prophet of the exile, Deutero-Isaiah. As such, they represent a mature expression of the Hebrew understanding of God. But it is my contention that Deutero-Isaiah's theology of God is a logical working out of elements that were present from Israel's exodus beginnings.

Furthermore, since our inquiry into Israel's story is for our purposes set within the framework of the Christian community and its story, we will ask whether and to what extent the two stories are one, and to what extent the Hebrew and the Christian notions of Covenant and Law are rooted in a shared vision of God.

What was the Hebrew God like? (1) He was God alone. (2) He was creator of the world and therefore (3) sovereign. (4) He was to be conceived of as a "living" God. Finally, (5) he was righteous or good. We will examine each of these affirmations below.

THE GOD WHO IS GOD ALONE

The Hebrews were monotheists. However, to assert this is not to resolve all questions regarding the sources or the point of origin of their exclusive monotheism.

Certainly the picture is far from clear with regard to the patriarchal narratives. The many designations for God in those narratives and the involvement of patriarchal existence in the polytheistic culture of its day cast doubt on any claims to an early, exclusive monotheism. But the thrust of the narratives, and especially the claim to a unique covenant relation between God and Israel, suggest a move toward exclusivism of devotion. Yet it could well be argued that the most we can claim for Abraham and his sons is a variety of *henotheism*. Henotheism is the term sometimes used to describe an intermediate stage between polytheism and monotheism in which exclusive devotion is demanded toward one god but without denying the existence of other gods worshiped by other tribes or nations.

Were the patriarchs henotheists? Nahum Sarna seems to be correct that the patriarchal accounts give no inkling of the struggle with paganism that is such a major theme of the exodus and post-exodus story.[1] The narratives concerning Abraham and his sons, as related in Genesis, do not display significant tension between the patriarchs and the surrounding society so far as religion is concerned. The matter of many versus the one God is simply not an issue. Such foreshadowing of a conflict in these accounts—for example, Jacob's discovery at Bethel that he could not limit his father's god to his father's tents—may be a reading back into the patriarchal story of the exodus experience.

But what of Moses? Was he a monotheist? It has been argued by no less a theologian than Sigmund Freud that Moses was in fact a henotheist, a view that Lester Meyer seems to support when he suggests that the first commandment "doesn't deny that there are other gods."[2] But Sarna rejects this contention. One of the distinguishing marks of the Sinai covenant, he argues, is its demand for the exclusive worship of one God."[3] By his judgment, "It is the arrival of Moses on the scene of history that heralds the first appearance of the notion of a war on polytheism."

Insofar as we can speak of Moses' personal understanding, since it comes to us filtered through the traditions of Israel, it seems safe to say that, while he might not have represented the refined and theoretical monotheism of a Deutero-Isaiah, we can call him, at least at this point, a *practical* monotheist. Whether Moses repudiated the existence of beings that other tribes or nations called gods, he stripped them of all power and significance. The account of the plagues in Exodus 7–11 presents Moses as striking a blow at the Egyptian pantheon or household of gods and demonstrating their ineptitude and impotence. He disempowers the gods of the Nile.

This is the point of the struggle of Moses with the Egyptian gods when he presents his challenge to Pharaoh. Thus, Yahweh, the God of the Hebrews, announces in Exodus 12:12, "I will mete out punishments to all the gods of Egypt, I the LORD." Whether their existence was theoretically denied is of minor import. Even if such beings were granted a shadowy existence as the foil against which the purposes of Yahweh would be displayed, they were reduced at the very least to the status of demons and at the most to nonentity. Compared to Yahweh they had no power, and in the final analysis what has no power has no being.

The Religious Meaning of Monotheism

We will explore the implications of Israel's monotheism more fully when we examine the first commandment. But a more general question needs to be addressed. We have suggested that a person's way of conceiving God has its impact on the way that person conceives life in general. What difference does monotheism make? Now, I am asking not merely about the numerical difference but the "religious" difference. However, in this case the two are not unrelated.

It has been observed that in important respects the difference between one and two is qualitatively greater than the difference between two and two million. In most languages there are two primary ways of expressing number: singular and plural. The singular form is used to designate oneness, that which is unique, that which stands alone; the plural is used to describe any other combination of entities up to infinity. Perhaps this state of affairs in our use of numbers reflects a valid insight, because once unity is broken or disintegrates into plurality it makes little difference what the number may become.

One of the stranger personality disorders with which people are afflicted is the condition sometimes called split or multiple personality. Those who suffer from such a personal disintegration bear witness to the agony and confusion of their condition. But one has to wonder whether the pain and confusion is greatly increased when the double personality becomes multiple, when two "selves" struggling within a single mind and body become many struggling selves. Is multiple personality inherently more pathological than a divided personality? Once the wholeness of the self has been ruptured even once it is gone, and with it the stability of life.

In even the more mature and structured expressions of polytheism, such as that in classical Greek mythology, we find a world lacking in fundamental unity. It is a world divided between the warring natural powers personified by the gods. There were gods of the heavens, the oceans, and the underworld beneath, gods of the sun and moon, of the four winds, of the forests, the meadows and the mountaintops. While these gods ultimately came to be arranged in a more or less ordered pantheon or "system" of greater and lesser deities, with a reigning god at the apex of the order, even that emperor god, Zeus, was far from sovereign and was able to exercise only limited dominion over his divine colleagues and even over his own consort.

Mortal life and expectations under such a system were highly unpredictable, since no one could anticipate which god or goddess at a given time would prevail. It was perhaps the longing for a sense of order and direction that led Greek religion to conceive the notion of the Fates, who controlled the destinies of the gods themselves! In the doctrine of the fates Greek polytheism seems to be a reaching out toward a proto-monotheism such as became a fact in Greek classical philosophy.

I am arguing here that Hebrew monotheism had little to do with number but was an assertion of the fundamental wholeness of things. Whatever powers there were in the world, they were subject to the all-governing power of the one God. Thus life in the world can take on meaning and nothing in principle is completely arbitrary. If *God* is one then *life* is one and human history makes sense.

THE GOD WHO CREATED THE WORLD

The biblical God is the creator God. This means among other things that he cannot be conceived, like the Greek gods, to be a part of the created order. The Hebrew war against idolatry was in part an assertion of God's independence over the world. This is the root of the powerful taboo against "graven images." God is not to be represented by anything in creation—not by a lion or a tree, not by the sun, not even by the loftiest of creatures, a human being—for to seek to so represent God is to falsify his relationship to his world. The Greek gods were a part of the world and therefore subject to and under the control of the larger system. Their power was checked and counterchecked by other gods and above all by the system itself. The gods had a beginning and would have an end. The biblical God stands in a very different relationship to the created order. It is *his* order. It is subject to *him*; he is not subject to it!

It is clear that when the Hebrew spoke of God as creator he was not talking merely or even mainly of origins. He was talking about the continuing relationship of creator and creation. Thus to speak of God as creator of the world had a double reference, much as do words such as "mother" and "father" at the human level. There are in the world today four people who call me father. When they do so they are saying something about origins—about the role I played in their biological beginnings—but I flatter myself that I hear much more when one of my sons or daughters says "This is my father." They speak of a continuing relationship of trust and support that, far more than the act of generation in which I took part once upon a time, gives the word its richness and power. So while the act of generation is now a dead fact of the past, my fatherhood is a living reality. There are indeed men who are fathers in the former sense that do not deserve to be so-called in the latter. By contrast, a dear friend of mine who was reared by two loving adoptive parents could speak of the man who, though having played no role in her generation, was a sustaining and loving presence in her life as her father.

The Hebrew conceived God's creativity as continual and sustaining. God was at all times actively upholding his creatures, so that if he should, even for a moment, withhold his presence they would cease to be. So the psalmist expresses it: "When you take our breath away, we die and return to dust!" (Ps 104:29).

THE GOD WHO IS SOVERIGN

The sovereignty of God is a conclusion following inexorably from his singularity and his creativity. As the only God and the source of all, no rival force or being can frustrate his purposes for his world. So once again, the Hebrew affirms the order and reliability of the world under God. *It* is ultimately *under* control because *he* is *in* control. We will consider in a later place whether that sovereignty was conceived of as a universal determination of all things by God or whether it allowed room for the free decisions and self-determinations of his creatures.

Now, these three affirmations—that God is God alone, that he is creator of the world and not a part of it, and that he is sovereign—constitute an impressive picture, but they fall short of exhausting the content of the biblical

God. A God so described is power but without determinate character. Above all, such a God lacks any of the moral dimensions that could define him as the covenant God. He could in fact be a demon. More remains to be said.

THE "LIVING GOD"

"The LORD is the true God; he is the living God and the everlasting King" (Jer 10:10). The words are from the late prophetic tradition of Israel, but the description of Yahweh as "Living God" occurs throughout the Old Testament literature from post-exodus times on (see Josh 3:10, Deut 5:26, Ps 42:2, Hos 1:10). I have framed the phrase "Living God" in quotation marks to call attention to its linguistic character. To speak of God as living is to employ the literary device of *metaphor*. Increasingly the metaphorical character of all language is being recognized. By employing the devices that in high-school English we learned to call *metaphor* and *simile*, we describe the unfamiliar in terms of the familiar.

A metaphor or a simile is a literary comparison. I might use metaphor to give you insight into the character and appearance of a friend. Suppose I tell you "Clifford is a great bear of a man." You would probably seize upon elements in your mental image of a bear to form an impression of Clifford: large, burly, perhaps a bit brusque. You would thereby be in possession of an element of truth about my friend. You would know him better than you had before. But a metaphor is not an identity! To speak of my friend as a great bear is not to suggest that he is like a bear in every respect—that he has fur and hibernates in winter.

Metaphorical language is *non*-literal; it falsifies even as it affirms. Thus for the Hebrew to speak of God as "living" is to employ language in a non-literal way. Every literally living creature is situated in time and place; it is born and it dies and it suffers all the slings and arrows to which flesh is heir. None of these statements can be applied without qualification to God.

Now, lest it be concluded that such non-literal, even physical, language is the product of primitive imagination, it should be born in mind that the ancient Hebrew forbade all efforts to represent God by anything in creation. There is good evidence that the Israelite understood the metaphorical and non-literal character of his representation of God.

Is "Living God" Merely a Metaphor?

The question itself is misleading. To suggest that the phrase "living God" is non-literal or metaphoric is not to belittle it or to imply that literal meaning would be better. It is in the rich and evocative character of metaphor and symbol that the true power and meaning of religious language can be found. The theologian Paul Tillich often rebuked literal-minded people who asked him, "Is religious language merely a symbol?" He would reply, "We should never say 'merely a symbol'; we should always say, 'not *less* than a symbol.'"[4] This also means that the search for less metaphoric or less symbolic language in the search for biblical truth is usually religiously self-defeating.

It is often observed that the language of the Bible and especially that of the Old Testament is heavily *anthropomorphic*. The word literally means "man-formed." *Anthropomorphism* is the use of human descriptive language or human categories of thought to describe that which is not human, or to bestow on a nonhuman entity human characteristics. Such language may be applied non-literally but still meaningfully. For example, a poet may refer to an oak tree as "spreading her leafy arms to pray" or describe a mountain crag as "stolid and resolute." Such human language may also be used to give character or concreteness to realities that rise above the human realm, as when, with the poet, I tell you that "Smiling truth looks down upon her sons," or when I refer to God's mighty arm or his all-seeing eye.

Since metaphorical and especially anthropomorphic language arise from the human understanding, it is clear that such language falsifies even as it describes. Who would assume that the all-seeing eye of the Lord has lens and retina or is subject to myopia or astigmatism? Surely we do not mean to suggest such a thing. Thus the conclusion is sometimes drawn that we would serve God better if we could avoid such figurative or non-literal usage by systematically purging religious language of its anthropomorphic character.

The result is often the adoption of abstract language for God. God becomes "being itself," "ultimate reality," or, in Star Wars lingo, a faceless "Force" that is "with us." But does the retreat to abstraction escape from the ambiguity and bring us closer to the literal? Indeed, is there anything less literal than an abstraction? And is there anything more anthropomorphic? Nothing bears more surely the marks of the human mind and of human conceptualization than an abstraction. An oak tree has at least a measure of existence independent of the knower and describer, but one is not likely to find a green, nut-bearing abstraction growing in the same meadow.

To the layperson, this discussion may seem a strange and extended digression, but it has an important point. Tillich is surely right that *all* religious language is symbolic, just as in fact all language in general is symbolic. We must all use symbols, and the eternal struggle is to find symbols and metaphors that, either singly or in combination, best express the reality we have experienced. This is the point that needs to be understood. In fact, the ancient writers of Scripture seem to have understood it better than many of their latter-day interpreters. The question is never how literal the words were that they employed, but how expressive and how true they were to the reality they had come to know in living experience.

What we are saying is that the Hebrew understanding of God was not the result of disinterested speculation; it was forged in the crucible of oppression and deliverance. In choosing the metaphor "living" they knew well that they were falsifying in some measure. The word is organic, and the only literally living things within their experience were embodied things. God was not embodied! But they chose that metaphor, with all its liabilities, *because it expressed the deep essence of their encounter.* If it was misleading to call him living God, it would be far more misleading to call him "dead God"—another metaphor. Our purpose then is to unpack as best we can the meaning that the phrase "living God" contained for the Hebrew.

What Is a Living God Like?

What were the leading insights of their experience that prompted them to so describe him? What does living God imply? Three defining dimensions of the exodus God can be suggested. God is *personal, active,* and *purposive.* These three designations refer back to the divine self-manifestation as the Israelites experienced it in the exodus.

(1) *The Personal God.* Johnstone is surely correct when he observes that "*the self-disclosure of God* must be regarded as the central theme of the Exodus,"[5] and the divine self-disclosure that initiates the whole exodus narrative is recorded in dramatic detail in the "burning bush" event in Exodus 3 and 4. Central to the account of the burning bush is Moses' confrontation by God and the revealing of the divine name, Yahweh. Johnstone points out that while the *tetragrammaton,* or four-figure formula YHWH, is in the third person, Exodus 3:14 interprets it as first person. Accordingly, Yahweh is not an objective power or entity indirectly referred to as "he" or even "it," but the personal,

relational subject "I." God is not merely addressed as "Thou" but takes the initiative of addressing Moses as one person would address another.[6]

The personal nature of the Hebrew God is closely bound up with his character as the God of Covenants. His covenant with Israel, made first with the patriarchs and now renewed at Sinai, rests on the divine self-revelation. He enters into relation with a person (Moses) and with a people (Israel).

Covenants are by nature based on self-revelation, and self-revelation is the way in which people must be truly known. Things can be known by examination and, to a degree at least, their essence can be discovered. People must reveal themselves, as God does to Moses at Sinai. And, as in every true personal revelation, the epiphany itself is at the same time a concealment. The more that is known about an object, the less remains mystery. The more that is known of a person, the deeper and more awesome the mystery. So every revelation of the God of covenants is at the same time "a statement of God's being or action which veils the fullness of that being or action and safeguards the transcendence, otherness and freedom of God."[7]

If it is "anthropomorphic" to speak of God as *living*, how much greater are the problems involved in speaking of him as *person*, or even more, as *a* person? People are time-bound and embodied in ways that could not be appropriately applied to the creator God. But we should not make the mistake of thinking the Hebrew was unaware of this fact. On the contrary, God is continually spoken of in ways that qualify or limit the language of person. What, then, is the religious meaning of divine personhood in the Old Testament? Why does the Hebrew cling so tenaciously to the language of person, and why is God continually described in dramatic narrative as acting, thinking, deciding, committing, even regretting and repenting, as a finite personal being would do?

At the heart of this persistent personalism is the conviction that, whatever else he might or might not be, *God is the kind of God who enters into fellowship with men and women and so ratifies the value and meaning of human life*. The act of divine covenant-making is an act of human affirmation, just as affirmation is involved in the embracing of a child or a friend. So, in the covenant act, God embraced Israel, ratifying her worth and through her affirming the worth of human existence. Thus to speak of God as person is to affirm that human life and human values are not orphans in an essentially impersonal universe. Rather, personhood is rooted in the nature of things. It is not a cosmic accident or the chance outcome of a faceless and heartless process.

By its persistent and stubborn personalism, biblical religion sets itself against the kind of "cosmic masochism" sometimes manifest today in the scientific community. By the term masochism I mean a compulsion to self-belittlement or disparagement. Impressed by the immensity of the cosmos and the statistical preponderance of dead matter, and considering the vast expanse of cosmic time, scientists sometimes seem moved to dwell on the triviality and insignificance of human life and personal existence. The idea that selfhood has worth or special significance in the scheme of things is often dismissed as human arrogance. In contrast, the notion of a divine personhood is a challenge to the dogma assumed by such cosmic belittlement of the personal. It rejects the notion that significance and value can be calculated by mere statistics. The preponderance of inert soil granules is no sure evidence that soil is more significant than the single plant that draws nourishment from it. Similarly, it is possible that human personhood is statistically trivial and yet outweighs in worth the statistically preponderant. There is no direct correlation between statistics and worth.

The pastor of my youth, in response to a searching question, effectively shifted the frame of reference for this issue. He was asked, "Won't you acknowledge that, astronomically speaking, man is an insignificant speck?" He replied, "No, astronomically speaking, man is an *astronomer.*" He was agreeing with the personalism of thinkers like Alfred North Whitehead, Charles Hartshorne, and the philosophers of organism, according to whom every entity has its value, but *aware* entities—those with feeling, and especially those with self-consciousness and *self*-awareness—represent a higher level of nature and, at least possibly, of worth.[8]

Whatever else the biblical God is, he is the kind of being who is aware of and can enter into relationship with people, thereby ratifying and affirming the worth of their existence.

(2) *The Active God.* The biblical God is in no way subject to the ravages of time. He is, as regards his character, absolute and unchanging. But he is not frozen in the deep freeze of his own perfection.

Few misunderstandings of the Bible's intentions have had a more pernicious effect on Christian theology than confusing the divine stability and reliability with abstract and timeless perfection. This error has been abetted by the common translation of the divine name given to Moses at the burning bush. The name YHWH is commonly translated "I am." While this is a possible translation, the conclusion drawn from this translation is usually that of the utter timelessness of God and thus of his complete transcendence of the realm of time and history. Such a picture of God distorts the Hebrew understanding and has led to innumerable difficulties in Christian theology.

For the Old Testament, the notion of the invariability or unchangeability of God has little to do with whether God experiences time or has consciousness of a changing universe. The Hebrew God clearly is aware of and involved with the living world. The "timelessness" or "immutability" of God is not a theoretical or cosmological idea; it is a religious notion. Once again we must ask about a doctrine's religious meaning. Why was it critical for the Hebrew to affirm the unchangeability of God? The answer can be found only by remembering God's covenant promises to Israel.

Timelessness was a notion that would have scarcely had any meaning to the ancient Israelite. Reality *was* time, since it was history, and all things, especially humankind and God, were saturated by time. The point was whether history offered a hope that was trustworthy. As Sarna puts it, "This immutability provides inflexible reliability that the promise of redemption will be realized."[9]

The name YHWH, revealed at the burning bush, does indeed point to the character of God as *being*, but not in a sense that his being precludes his *becoming*. His stability and unchanging character is never seen as denying him access to the history of his people or compassion for their travails. It was never seen as preventing him from making himself felt in the events of the Hebrews' lives. If the biblical God can be spoken of as being, it is, in Sarna's words, "not being as opposed to non-being—not being as an abstract, philosophical notion—but being in the sense of God's active, dynamic presence.[10] He *is* because he is *there, then*, making his impact on time and history.

Perhaps a more accurate rendering of the name of God as given to Moses would put emphasis on this dramatic, time-involved God who enacts covenants and then brings them to fulfillment. If the name YHWH is understood as a third singular masculine imperfect verb with the prefix *ya*, then "the conjugation should be causative." This means, according to Johnstone, that "the name describes the activity of a creator god who *brings into being*."[11] So rather than reading the name as "I am" or "I am that I am," we should read it," I will cause to be."

Who then is confronting Moses in the bush and the pharaoh in Egypt and the people at Mount Sinai? It is the God who makes things happen, who "makes the fur fly." He is the active God.

(3) *The Purposive God.* God's activity is not random or undirected. He is not mere energy, expending itself in meaningless activity or exhausting itself in all directions like the glowing fragments of an exploding skyrocket. He is working out his purposes in the world, and the deepest meaning of the exodus for the

Hebrews is that they had been taken up in covenant with that God, and that they, mortal and unworthy as they were, had become partakers in that purpose.

We have spoken of the dramatic character of God. That sense of the divine drama received its impetus from the exodus experience, and it has shaped the entire biblical outlook. The meaningless comings and goings of history and its peoples are now given shape by the discernment of God's purposes within them, and that shape is defined by the covenant action of God. Israel's story has meaning and direction because of the covenant God.

Israel was sure that, when God's divine purpose was revealed by his gracious act in the exodus, she was able to begin to see in this redemptive deed his larger purposes in her whole history. And the implication of her history seemed to embrace, at least potentially, the history of humankind and even of creation itself. Thus the drama seemed to unfold to their understanding. To call it a divine drama is to banish any image of a disengaged and timeless God watching in serene detachment the meaningless scurrying of the creatures of time. He is actor and experiencer of the drama. It is also to reject any notion of random comings and goings. There was nothing random in the drama of the exodus. It had beginning, a development, and an ending. It was going somewhere! Its character was:

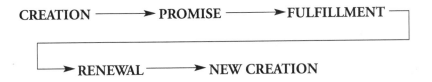

This dramatic scheme shapes the Hebrew and ultimately the Christian view of God and history. All Hebrew hope for the future depended on the faithfulness and the competence of Yahweh to fulfill his purposes. The name Yahweh has an inescapable forward thrust and is sometimes translated not "I am" but "I will be." If, as Johnstone suggests, this is the more natural rendering, then he is surely correct that "the statement is primarily soteriological," that is, it points to God's redemptive or saving intent, and as such, it is "a promise of continuing activity, even an eschatological affirmation."[12] The name Yahweh is not merely announcement or identity but *promise*.

Therefore, when the Hebrew speaks of God as the "living God," he is telling his story of epiphany, covenant, and hope for redemption. The personal, active, and purposive elements of the divine nature blend and reinforce each other in the telling of that story. No living God, no covenant! No covenant, no hope!

THE GOD WHO IS RIGHTEOUSNESS

We have attempted to understand the Hebrew vision of God as an unfolding of the exodus encounter, as born of the divine self-manifestation to Moses and subsequently to the people. By the nature of his presence and by his actions, they came to know this God as the one, creator, sovereign, and living God. But one more implication of that encounter alone could render God worthy of worship and a true covenant partner. Nothing has been said—except by implication—about the purposes that shape God's sovereign activity.

In other words, nothing that we have said to this point speaks to the question of God's moral character. He could in fact even yet be a demon. Men have conceived of malignant deities who for all their potency take pleasure in the pain of their creatures. A malignant god, or even a morally neutral god, might be feared or respected, but could such a god be the object of worship? Could such a god be worthy of the adoration extended to him in biblical faith? Richard Niebuhr is surely right that the ultimate test of a revelation is its power to move us to worship.[13] Before we can speak of the biblical God, more needs to be said. And the Hebrews said it; in the wake of the exodus they came to speak of God as *righteous.*

The hebrew word *tsedeq,* usually rendered *righteous,* originally had no moral connotation, signifying only that which conforms to the norm. Thus a person or a thing could be judged righteous insofar as he, she, or it was consistent, or more accurately, *self-*consistent. Such a neutral designation would provide little insight into the actual character of the one designated. But to use the word out of rich, firsthand experience would be a different matter. The word righteous would then take on a qualitative significance and meaning.

An example may be needed here. For me to speak of my wife as consistent is to speak out of a half-century of living. As a mere husband, I have long ago given up any hope of predicting her. Whatever I anticipate is apt to be frustrated in the realization; yet I am able to live confidently because I have come to know the wholeness and the steadiness of the character that underlies her often surprising acts. I do not know in any given instance what she will do— this is part of her charm—but I know that it will be at heart a manifestation of the goodness and love that never fails of expression.

When the Hebrew spoke of the righteousness of God, the word was filled with meaning by their experience of his mighty acts of calling and covenant and deliverance. He was the kind of God who had called them into being, saved them from assimilation or annihilation in Egypt, and overshadowed them with his presence and love. Therefore the word took on ethical and even soteriological and eschatological meaning. Alan Richardson has indicated that the word in its Old Testament usage "gradually develop[s] . . . toward the meaning of benevolence, salvation."[14] It came to mean that the purpose the living God was bringing about by his covenant activity toward Israel was the salvation of his people. His purposes were never malignant, always benign and redemptive. In a word, he is *good*.

NOTES

[1] Nahum Sarna, *Exploring Exodus: The Heritage of Biblical Faith* (Napierville IL: Alec R. Allenson, Inc., 1965), 144.

[2] Lester Meyer, *The Message of Exodus* (Minneapolis: Augsburg Publishing House, 1983), 122.

[3] Sarna, *Exploring Exodus*, 122.

[4] Paul Tillich, *Dynamics of Faith* (New York: Harper Torchbooks, Harper and Brothers Publishers, 1957), 45.

[5] W. Johnstone, *Exodus* (Sheffield England: JSOT Press, 1990), 105.

[6] Ibid., 104.

[7] Ibid., 105.

[8] Sarna, *Exploring Exodus*, 52.

[9] Ibid.

[10] Johnstone, *Exodus*, 103.

[11] Ibid., 104.

[12] Ibid.

[13] H. Richard Niebuhr, *The Meaning of Revelation* (New York: Collier Books, Macmillan Publishing Company, 1960), 104.

[14] Alan Richardson, ed., *A Theological Word Book of the Bible* (New York: Macmillan Company, 1960), 202.

Chapter Three

⌒

Humankind, Community, and History

The one, sovereign, living, righteous God who brought all the worlds into being called Israel into covenant with himself. So goes the story that Israel learned to tell. At the beginning of the previous chapter, we suggested that a person's understanding of God tends to shape that person's perspective on every aspect of life in the world. We also suggested that the Hebrews, who at first shared the outlook and worldview common to their age, began, in the wake of the exodus, to take on a distinctiveness that eventually set them apart from their neighbors.

It is at least plausible that this distinctiveness is a factor in their national persistence on the stage of history. This people—almost uniquely among the nations of the ancient Near East—were to persist as a recognizable people, while their neighbors were to vanish from the stage of history. Of all the peoples of the ancient Near East who have left traces of their existence in history, Israel alone is present in recognizable form today. In other words, this growing distinctiveness may have had a measure of survival power in it.

If there was such a transformative power in the covenant consciousness and in the view of God it engendered, then it would have influenced every aspect of the people's life and faith. No doubt those differences were often matters of degree, and our limited knowledge of their contemporaries prevents us from saying whether and to what extent their neighbors might have shared this or that insight. But the Hebrew vision seems to have rested less in the specific differences than in the creative interaction of these new insights and intuitions. What especially interests us is to discover gradually emerging and increasingly distinctive ways of looking at their world. Then we ask whether they shaped the development of later Hebrew history, the Christian faith and, in significant respects, the Western world.

We will examine in this brief chapter three aspects of that emerging outlook we will call biblical. We will suggest that gradually and in the most intense struggle, Israel developed new ways of looking at humanity, of understanding human community, and of assessing the nature, meaning, and value of history.

Our purpose is not merely to describe the emerging Hebrew understanding of humankind, community, and history, but to see the relationship between these ways of seeing and the view of God we described previously. We will then suggest ways in which these understandings emerged from the exodus experience.

A NEW VIEW OF HUMANKIND

A person's self-image is significantly shaped by the relationships within which he or she lives. It is not surprising then that a people such as the Hebrews, in the light of the great encounter of the exodus and the new and living relationship with God that resulted, reexamined their existence in the world. It is not surprising that they asked new and searching questions about their status and worth before God.

If we take the Hebrew story seriously, we can detect a gradually emerging and distinctive view of humankind. It is, in fact, a strange and paradoxical view that at face value seems to combine mutually exclusive and contradictory elements. Yet, when viewed with an eye toward universal experience, it could be argued that such a view of humanity is experientially undeniable. The Hebrew view of humankind holds in tension a new sense of human worth and a deepened sense of human unworthiness. At the same time, the status of the race seems to have been immeasurably heightened and greatly depreciated; the human stock shot up even as fell to new lows. How did this strange assessment come about?

In the story related in 1 Samuel of David's secret anointing at Bethlehem, we are told that Samuel presented himself unheralded at the door of David's father Jesse. One can only wonder what thoughts or emotions arose in Jesse when he found the high priest of all Israel on his doorstep, but his response to that presence is amusing: "Comest thou *peaceably?*" he asked. Now consider what may have been the complex mixture of emotions and perceptions that arose when Israel began to internalize the meaning of exodus: "God has confronted us and *entered into our history. Cometh he peaceably?*"

Imagine that you receive a telephone call from the highest levels of government and are summoned into conversation with the chief executive himself. Suppose the message from the president is as follows: "We are searching for someone to undertake a critical mission on which the peace of the world may depend, someone in whom all the parties involved in these delicate negotiations can have confidence. Your name has been given to us and all our studies have affirmed you for the task. Will you accept this mission?"

What would be the typical reaction to such a call? The first response would certainly be disbelief, but suppose the genuineness of the proposal is beyond doubt? Would not most of us be filled with profoundly conflicting emotions? Would not our sense of worth be in that moment immeasurably elevated, to have received such trust and honor? "Have I not been made the colleague and confidant of the president himself?" If this were my experience, I would find it impossible not to view myself in a new light. "How about that?" I would surely ask. "I must have impressed someone; I must have hidden virtues that I little suspected. Imagine! Me!" I would feel profoundly honored by the offer. Yet, at the same moment my sense of inadequacy would overwhelm me. "Who? Me? Not me! Anyone but me!"

Israel responded in this way to her sense of covenant calling. Her confrontation with God and her inclusion within his purposes and love seem to have heightened her sense of worth and deepened her sense of sin! It was an awesome thing to become the people of God.

The patriarchal motif of which we spoke above—the contrast between the faithfulness of God and the faithlessness of the patriarchs—expresses this paradox of humankind. Israel was unworthy of God's covenant; yet she was continually astonished at his gracious calling and his steadfast love. "Why us?" they continually asked. "Who are we that we are worthy of such honor and of such a calling? Our father was a wandering Aramean."

It is certain that this complementary, yet contrasting consciousness of richness and poverty, enhancement and degradation altered their sense of themselves; but only secondarily and belatedly did they consider what it meant for the family of humankind. The Hebrews were not generalists in the modern sense. But their understanding of themselves as honored by God and yet unworthy of his honor had universal possibilities. The care with which the post-exodus law addressed the needs of the "strangers within the gates" suggests that the covenant even early on had larger meaning than just Israel.

It remained for the universal dimensions of the covenant to be developed by the mature prophets and by the Christian community. Perhaps the clearest expression of this universalizing is in the encounter of Simon Peter with the Roman centurion (Acts 10). At least by implication, their sense of themselves as the happy but unworthy heirs of God's grace was capable of describing a larger human community than that of Israel alone.

The strange paradoxical picture of humankind—would we do better to call it dialectical?—is reflected in the pre-patriarchal story in Genesis 1. It should be remembered that this telling of the creation story—the so-called "Priestly" account—was written long after the exodus and, according to most scholars, represents the period of the Babylonian exile (586–538 BC). This would make it contemporary with the warm, universal vision of Isaiah. It is certain that nowhere in the Hebrew Scriptures is there a more mature expression of the view of humankind than we are describing than in the writings of this latter-day prince of Hebrew prophesy.

Genesis 1 preserves the tension of worthy and unworthy in the "image of God" metaphor. As the purpose and climax of creation, humankind is likened unto God himself. We stand above the rest of creation and are indeed only a little lower than the angels. Most significant, the freedom and self-consciousness that are human because of this special nature make us creators in our own right. Neither our opposable thumbs nor our erect posture sets us apart from even the loftiest animals. Our power to bring about the new sets us apart.

This is why humans have dimensions of existence either vestigial or unknown in the animals. Only human beings have culture and history. Culture is nature transformed by the creativity of humankind. When the climate plunges into an ice age, whole animal species perish. Men and women discover fire and build snug houses. So by human creativity, a whole new dimension of the world has come to be.

Those like the historian Lynn White, who have in recent decades excoriated the biblical notion of the image of God as self-serving flattery have not given adequate heed to Genesis.[1] The metaphor "image of God" is a cold-sober and frighteningly realistic view of the human species. Far from being shallow self-flattery, it is a solemn warning. Being in the image of God is a daunting thing. It is no wonder that men and women have sometimes longed for the simplicity of the merely animate or even the inanimate. So Walt Whitman could write, "I think I could turn and live with the animals . . . they are so placid and so self-contained. They do not sweat and whine about their condition, they do not lie awake in the dark and weep for their sins."[2]

The poet is, of course, correct; the animals have no sins to weep for or repent from. But they also have no passion, no joy, no regrets—indeed, no poetry and no poets. The capacity for regret makes the sweat and agony and tears of guilt real, as well as the power of self-alienation and self-destruction.

The pathos of Victor Hugo's twisted Quasimodo well expresses the vulnerability to a kind of pain that seems uniquely human. In the final scene of the motion picture adaptation of the novel, the hunchback sees his beloved Esmeralda in the arms of another. Racked by the burden of human love in a twisted body, he embraces the grotesque gargoyle on the cathedral parapet and cries, "Why was I not made of stone like thee?"[3]

The message of Genesis is that being in God's image is a two-edged sword. We humans can bring about the new, create community and love, compose eloquent poetry and music, build monuments to heroism and virtue, and do all manner of things of which no other creature is capable. We can even dream of heaven. Above all, as the climax of a creation called "good," we are somehow the *highest* good.

Precisely because we are so exalted above the beasts, we can also sink to levels unknown to them. We can create garbage dumps and nuclear devastation. We are capable of exquisite and calculated evil that no baser creature could envision. As we can exalt, so can we also debase. Indeed, because we are *like* God, we can begin to think that we *are* God. Because humankind alone of all creatures has the freedom and the power to corrupt God's created goodness, we are not merely the most exalted good but also most depraved and extravagant evil—indeed, the only true evil. Without the latter, we could not be the former.

Both the high status and value of the person and the deep sense of human sin that characterize biblical religion as a whole are rooted in this awareness of the creator God who has embraced humankind in his grace. The much older account of creation in Genesis 2 reflects this dialectical view of humankind in a slightly different way. Humankind is formed from the soil; thus we are part of the earth, and whenever we forget that fact we are reminded by arthritis, infection, or death. Yet of all creatures we alone have received the breath of God himself.

The persistent themes of failure, grace, and renewal throughout the Old Testament are rooted in this sense of unworthiness and yet acceptance, experienced, so to speak, "in the face of God." The classic account of standing before God in dread and grace is that of the prophet Isaiah before the temple. To confront the worthiness and the power of God is to be reduced to utter worthlessness ("Woe is me, for I am undone!" [Isa 6:5]). But, as the prophet discovers, behind the divine "No!" is the divine "Yes!" To confront God in his faithfulness and his love, even in the terror of judgment, is to be called to acceptance and worth.

THE INTEGRITY OF BIBLICAL HUMANITY

We must take care, though, not to be misunderstood when we speak of these two aspects of human nature. The Hebrew understanding of humankind is no dualism! What we have called the paradox of humankind should not be confused with the popular notion that the human being is made up of two separable elements, body and mind (or soul). Such dualistic thinking is on the whole foreign to biblical religion, except perhaps in some of the latter-day expressions of Hebraism under the influence of Persian or Greek thought. The Hebrew did not think of a human being as consisting of two separate elements, body and spirit, but rather as a "psychosomatic" unity. Whatever is true of body is true likewise of spirit. Therefore to speak of the paradox of worth and unworth does not mean an evil, corruptible body and a good, incorruptible soul. It is not my body that is corrupt and unworthy; it is I! It is not my soul and spirit that is precious to the creator; it is I!

Biblical religion views the person as a psychosomatic unity. This is why the notion of immortality as a disembodied soul is less biblical than the notion of a resurrection. Thus whatever is true of any part of me is likewise true of all of me. Am I sinful? It isn't only my flesh that is the problem; it is my whole being, flesh and spirit as one. Am I worthy of God's concern and love? If so, it is not my "soul"—the notion of a disembodied soul is Greek, not Hebrew—but *me* that he embraces and loves. *I* am lofty and lowly, saint and sinner.

I have belabored this point because I have found it uncommonly difficult for modern Christian people to escape the metaphysical dualism that has affected our thinking about our own natures, with profound consequences for our theology.

THE PRACTICAL IMPLICATIONS
OF THE HEBREW VIEW OF HUMANKIND

Humankind, then, is a dialectic tension of worth and worthlessness. Such a dynamic and dialectical understanding of the human situation appears to fly in the face of simpler and more coherent views of human nature, but it has deep correspondence with human experience. It is not too much to say that wherever it has been taken seriously it has provided a needed corrective to two dangerous oversimplifications of human nature. I refer to all forms of idealism that dismiss a person's capacity for evil or attribute evil to forces outside the self, and to all forms of naturalism or materialism that ignore a peron's capacity for self-transience, creativity, and love. The first can be labeled "blue-eyed optimism," the second "black-eyed cynicism."

Most varieties of optimistic idealism, including many forms of social and political liberalism, fail to take seriously the darker side of human possibility. The consequence is that they are unprepared to confront the darkness within the soul and within society. Whenever the unqualified goodness of the self is assumed, then the failure of human community leads to scapegoating.

In the musical *South Pacific*, Oscar Hammerstein has Lieutenant Cable express such a philosophy:

You've got to be taught to hate and fear,
You've got to be taught from year to year,
It's got to be drummed in your dear little ear,
You've got to be carefully taught . . .
You've got to be taught before it's too late,
Before you are six or seven or eight.
To hate all the people your relatives hate.[4]

While this philosophy recognizes a truth—the way in which one generation influences another and the resulting social solidarity of sin—it draws a dangerously naive conclusion. Optimism believes that social evil could be eliminated by better teaching or by removing evil influences that are foreign to "good" human nature. The evil or nefarious influence might be the "older generation" ("We the young didn't create this mess!") or the "few bad apples in the barrel," or paradoxically those who hold or teach doctrines we hate. Such optimists about human nature usually remain unaware of the possibility that the evil propaganda of one generation flourishes because it falls on fertile soil.

In other words, Hammerstein is wrong about the *origin* of societal evil. It is true that hate finds its *focus* in parents and society but not its *origin*. We don't have to be taught to hate; this capacity is rooted in our finitude and vulnerability as creatures who are not God. What family and society teach us is *who* or *what* to hate. Failure to understand this is to invite disillusionment and despair.

It is also an invitation to divide the world into warring communities of good and evil rather than understanding that all partake of both.

The tragedy of a naive humanism that assumes the goodness of humankind without serious qualifications is that it is always surprised by human reality. The disillusionment that follows such surprise is the fruit of naive optimism gone sour. This has surely been the case in the West in the last three centuries; the collapse of Enlightenment humanistic society, the submergence of optimistic laissez-faire capitalism into the brutality and economic opportunism of modern industrialism, and the descent of optimistic Marxian communism into the unspeakable horrors of Stalinism are all illustrations. All failed not because they were too cynical but because at heart they were too naive. They were uncritically optimistic about human possibilities.[5]

Therefore, blue-eyed optimism tends to collapse into its opposite, which in its more despairing forms is the kind of "black-eyed cynicism" reflected in William Steig's famous cartoon. It shows a little man cowering in the corner of a box, muttering, "People are no damn good!" In its less despairing form, such cynicism finds expression in various kinds of territorial conflict or political opportunism, life being "every man (or every tribe, family, or nation) for himself."

The biblical human is neither saint—having, as he does, the power within him to distort and corrupt the best in himself or in the world—nor is he a "naked ape"—having, as he does, the power to rise above his animal nature to achieve creativity, community, and even selfless love. Any realistic expectation must take both into account.

A NEW VIEW OF COMMUNITY

Covenant gives birth to community, and the community takes on the character of the covenant-making experience. Whatever kind of Israelite community existed in Egypt before the exodus we can know only in a sketchy way. Israel's story scarcely comments on the centuries of Egyptian settlement. What little we can discern strongly suggests a people in the process of losing their distinctive identity and dangerously near to being absorbed by the dominant culture. The deliverance of the exodus was less a deliverance from physical extirpation than from assimilation.

The shared experience of the exodus, the conviction of divine epiphany, and the sense of national destiny to which these gave rise never completely deserted Israel. But from these exodus years, she struggled to define the nature of the resulting community. Was she to be another migrant nation in a world awash with such, seeking after land and wealth and political dominion? Or was there within the exodus experience the raw material for a new and more embracing kind of community? I suggest that such raw material was provided by the understanding of God that grew out of their covenant experience

THE BOND OF COMMUNITY

Human community presupposes bonds. Even the most minimal or fragmentary community exists because of some quality of mutuality, something possessed in common by all the members. The first significant community that most of us know is the family, which rests on the multiple bonds of blood, tradition, and mutual interdependence. Within the history of community— whether family, neighborhood, church, nation, club, fraternity, or common interest—the complex of mutual bonds grows ever richer and more determinative for the members with the passing of time.

If a child lacks significant participation in a community that shapes self-identity and provides a home for values, that child may fail to develop a full humanity. If a person is deprived of a community that supports his or her selfhood and gives it meaning—for example, by the death of a loved one or the destruction of a family unit, by social ostracism or by solitary confinement—the identity structure of the individual may disintegrate or collapse. Therefore, participation in a living community and the sharing of its constitutive bonds are critical to human health and freedom.

But there is a negative aspect of community that is a source of profound evil and misery. Human communities by their nature are exclusive. In order to define and protect our community, we must exclude those who do not share our defining bond or characteristic. Thus the warmth of belonging tends to be balanced by the chill of exclusion and the pain or isolation for those who do not belong. In order to include us within the group we must, in Sam Goldwyn's words, "Include them out!"

This exclusive nature of human communities is a major root of human conflict, whether class, religious, racial, or other. The irony is that the deep need for acceptance and identity that a community provides fuels at the same time fear of its loss and leads to the fragmentation of humanity. The community identity that for one is a symbol of confident selfhood can be for another a symbol of exclusion, resentment, and hatred.

If the bonds that ordinarily constitute communities are divisive and destructive of a larger whole, is it possible that there could be a nonexclusive community? Again I am suggesting that there was in the Hebrew understanding of God the seeds for such a community.

It is certainly true that these seeds were slow to sprout and to take root in the history of Israel and even slower to bring forth mature fruit. No problem was to prove more intransigent and resistant to solution in the history of Israel, and indeed, in the biblical tradition as a whole, than the question of particularism versus universalism. Does the covenant community of God embrace Israel alone, or is it, at least in principle, intended for humanity? What indeed is the status of the "stranger within the gates" or of those peoples the Hebrews designated "the nations"? Was it possible that the Israelite could address the Egyptian, the Moabite, and the Philistine as brother?

Not even the gradually enlarging visions of the great prophets of the exile could win a clear victory for universalism over particularism, as is witnessed to by the narrow legalism and xenophobia of the post-exilic period. On what grounds could all peoples be brothers and sisters? Through much of Israel's history, it is doubtful that this question would find an answer.

Nevertheless, if it is true that the Christian community was to embrace haltingly but truly a more inclusive perspective, it was not without grounds for doing so in the faith of Israel. The warrant for an inclusive community coextensive with humankind was there from the exodus on. It lay in the character of the covenant God. The logic is never more clearly set forth than by Isaiah: If God is God alone, the creator of the world, then he is the creator and God of Gentile and Hebrew alike. He is everybody's God. If he is indeed "a righteous God and a savior," then can the conclusion be avoided? "Come unto me, *all ye ends of the earth*, for I am God and there is no other" (Isa 45:22).

It is not unreasonable to see this sweeping announcement of an all-embracing human community as the logical outgrowth of the character of the covenant God. It was a community that need not exclude either black or white, Gentile or Jew, male or female, as Isaiah saw it in the sixth century BC and as the Apostle Paul saw it in the first century AD. Whatever may separate individuals and societies, the reality of a common origin in the creative act of God overarches and encompasses such differences.

A NEW VIEW OF HISTORY

Western history is essentially linear. I will occasionally call upon a student to come to the board, take chalk in hand, and draw a "picture" of history. Invariably such a student will draw a "time line," since this is the way specific periods of history are represented in high school or college history classes. In so doing, both the students and their teachers reflect the influence of the Judeo-Christian story on Western civilization in general.

The progressive outlook of Western history as well as its dynamism and forward momentum—whether for good or evil—owes much to the biblical view of a God who shapes time for the fulfillment of his purposes. While generalizations are risky, especially regarding the times of Israel's origins, it seems likely that the cultures in which her drama unfolded were for the most part cyclical in their thinking about time. Beyond that, many—perhaps most—of the cultures of the ancient world were also cyclical in their understanding of the ordering of history. Time was seen as moving in a circular way. The roots of such cyclical thinking are not difficult to discern; the patterns of nature, at least insofar as they can be recognized within the span of a lifetime, seem to be repetitive. Day follows night and night day. Spring and summer, autumn and winter, seedtime and harvest, birth, growth, maturity, reproduction, death—all come and go in seemingly endless repetition. The image of the "circle of time" is a commonplace of archeological investigation.

The problem inherent in a cyclical view of time and history—at least as seen through Western eyes—is the absence of a sense of historical meaning and significance. Cyclical history is history devoid of purpose since the essence of the cycle is repetition. Nothing that transpires in the course of history, none of the mighty acts of prophets or kings, none of the day-to-day decisions of men and women, ever change things for good. What *has been* once more *is,* and will be again. The events of history are deprived of permanent significance. It is not uncommon for cultures based on the cyclical image to be characterized by stability and lack a deep sense of forward movement. Such cultures are apt to be static rather than dynamic, and religions that view the world cyclically are apt to find meaning not in the events of time but in the timeless realm of the eternal.

Such, to be sure, was the case in late Greek transcendent monism, which has its classical expression in Plato. Such is also generally the case in the India-born religions such as Hinduism, so that rebirth on the wheel of Karma, with its endless comings and goings, is not viewed as a desirable thing. In religions that teach the doctrine of reincarnation or the transmigration of the soul, the goal of the adherent is *not* to be reincarnated; rather, the devotee seeks deliverance from the wheel and from the endless repetitions it brings. This is why the notion of reincarnation, whatever its value, should not be confused with the notion of resurrection or immortality in Western religions, both of which imply not an endless repetition but some kind of consummation or fulfillment.

There is no reason to doubt that the ancestors of the Hebrews shared the widespread cyclical view of history prior to the exodus. But there is every reason to see in the exodus a radical confrontation with time and history. It transformed their way of looking at the world and acting in it. They found themselves in company with "the God Who Acts," a living God who was shaping time according to his purposes.[6] This, then, was history that had movement and direction, and this sense of a divine purposive activity unrolled the cycle of history. The cycle became an arrow. Time became unidirectional and implied some meaningful hope and consummation. Biblical history is "going somewhere."

Because Israel found herself experiencing this new linear time and sharing in God's directed history, her every act and decision was filled with new meaning. The events of the exodus changed everything henceforth. Nothing could ever be the same. Nothing could ever again be sheer repetition. Israel's sense of history as purposive is deeply rooted in her sense of a purposive God, and it is profoundly formative of the Western sense that the events of history move us ever onward. We may visualize history as an arrow, as suggested above, or we may opt for some other model that acknowledges its complexity—perhaps a spiral, which allows for repetitions that are yet part of a forward process. In any case, at the heart of any model of history we adopt must be the sense of purpose that draws its power from the God who acts.

NOTES

[1] Lynn White, *Machina Ex Deo: Essays in the Dynamism of Western Culture* (Cambridge MA and London England: M.I.T. Press, 1968). See especially the essay "The Historical Roots of our Ecological Crisis," 75-94.

[2] Walt Whitman, *Song of Myself* 32, lines 1-6, in *The Portable Walt Whitman*, ed. Mark Van Doren and Malcolm Cowley (New York: Penguin Books, U.S.A., Inc., 1973), 64-65.

[3] Victor Hugo, *The Hunchback of Notre Dame*. Motion picture version by R. K. O. Radio Pictures.

[4] Oscar Hammerstein II, *South Pacific* (New York: Williamson Music, Inc), 144-46.

[5] Reinhold Niebuhr taught a generation of theologians, historians, and sociologists to take seriously man's capacity both for justice and for evil. What we are calling a paradoxical view of humankind owes much to his interpretation of Genesis 1 and 2. See his definitive treatment and its warning against optimism and cynicism in his Gifford Lectures: Reinhold Niebuhr, *The Nature and Destiny of Man* (New York: C. Scribner's Sons, 1953). For his treatment of Marxism as an idealistic optimism, see his *The Children of Light and the Children of Darkness* (New York: C. Scribner's Sons, 1972).

[6] G. Earnest Wright, *The Book of the Acts of God* (Garden City NY: Anchor Books, Doubleday & Company, Inc., 1960), 25.

Chapter Four

❧

The Covenant
and the Law

In the previous chapters, we sought to understand the theme that perhaps more than any other gives shape and substance to the Hebrew story—the theme of covenant—and we attempted to see that theme as emerging from the exodus experience of Israel. We also argued that much of the distinctiveness of the Hebrew outlook was rooted, at least in large measure, in that experience. Now we need to ask about the relation of the covenant motif to another motif that has been formative in the history of Israel, of the Christian tradition, and of Western society as a whole. I refer to the tradition of Torah, or law.

THE COVENANT AS REVELATION

We have affirmed that for the Hebrew the covenant arose from God's self-revelation. But what kind of event can truly be judged a revelation? What distinguishes a true event of revelation from other events that awaken strong emotions or impress us with their solemnity? According to H. Richard Niebuhr, a true revelation has the following marks:[1]

) It shines by its own light. An event is truly revelatory for an individual or for a people if it requires no validation but its own reality and power. It is *self-authenticating.* If one can ask why a particular event, insight, or experience should be considered a revelation, then it is not truly revelatory after all, because it must be explained and illuminated by some other, more trustworthy light. One cannot go back behind a true revelation to find a prior reason for its truth.

This is why there are no convincing arguments for the trustworthiness of a proposition or a faith. This is why one cannot finally prove the reality of God or the truth of an epiphany. One person might lead another by persuasion to *confront* an epiphany, but in the final moment all arguments are reduced to silence. Either the revelation seizes the newcomer, in which case all arguments and proofs become superfluous, or it does not, in which case they are useless. This witness either says, "Yes! Of course!" or walks away. A revelation must shine by its own light or not at all.

(2) *It illumines everything else in our experience.* This means that a true revelation casts the light of understanding on ourselves and everything else in our lives. It cannot itself be further explained, but it "explains" or gives meaning to everything else. A revelation is transformative, and it becomes the key for reinterpreting our place in the world and in history. In the light of such a moment, our past is subject to new scrutiny and comes to carry new meaning. It also provides the way for understanding our present. This means our total present, in all its dimensions—not merely our personal present! Rather, it ties our present to the shared present of the community and the world. Finally, a true revelation brings meaning into the otherwise aimless sequence of events we call our history. In other words, it provides a basis for anticipation, for hope, for a future.

Thus every true revelation binds together remembrance and anticipation. The genesis of every "story" is revelation. If what we have said previously is an accurate retelling of the Hebrew story, then it is a fitting example of Niebuhr's model. The manifestation of God to Moses at the burning bush and the adventure of epiphany and covenant-making that followed became the defining event of Israel's history. As such, it required no external ratification. It shone by its own light.

The centrality of the exodus event is abundantly attested in Israel's subsequent history. Its importance can be seen from the volume of materials dedicated to it. The brief half-century that embraces deliverance, law-giving, and entrance into the land is chronicled by four large books of the Pentateuch—the books of Exodus, Leviticus, Numbers, and Deuteronomy—while the whole of prior human and cosmic history is chronicled in only one—Genesis. The centrality of the exodus is revealed by the place it held in Israel's subsequent history. The remainder of the Old Testament is haunted by and shaped by the experience of the exodus. Ronald Clements comments on "the immense importance attached by the pre-exilic prophets to the traditions of the covenant in Israel. The repeated allusions to the election of Israel at the exodus . . . bear witness to the determinative significance of Israel's covenant status as the people of Yahweh . . . [and of] Yahweh's gracious calling of the people out of servitude into the freedom of his service."[2] Similarly, Nahum Sarna calls the exodus "the pivotal event" and "the dominant theme in Israelite history."[3]

The exodus became for the Hebrews the key for reunderstanding their patriarchal and even pre-patriarchal past. In the exodus experience, and only in it, Israel was able to give structure and meaning to the memories that predated the deliverance from Egypt. And in the light of deliverance and covenant, she was inspired to put her patriarchal origins in the larger framework of world history.

EXODUS AND CREATION

It was the character of God as revealed in the exodus that led the Israelites to the other great theme of their story: creation. We have spoken above of the biblical God as a creator God. Sarna has written that "Biblical religion revolves around two themes, creation and the Exodus." The first, Sarna adds, "asserts God's undivided sovereignty over nature, the latter his hegemony over history."[4] But the Israelites' confidence that God was Lord of nature rested on their conviction that God had acted in history—in the exodus.

Theologian Friedrich Schleiermacher reminds us that the Christian doctrine of creation cannot stand on its own as a primary doctrine, whatever its importance, because we have no direct experience of beginnings.[5] This is true even of personal beginnings, but it is even more true of world and cosmic origins. Thus the Christian affirmation of God as creator of the world arises out of the experience of redemption and sovereign love—that is out of *election*.

Schleiermacher's insight is a warning that we must not lose the religious substance of the doctrine of creation or convert this great confession into a pseudo-scientific dogma about how the world got here. It must not be mistaken for a metaphysical, or worse, a scientific dogma. The biblical doctrine of creation is not a cosmology. Whenever Christians try to convert it into a theory of world origins, they are invariably embarrassed by the inexorable progress of science. But—and this is more serious—they lose its real religious meaning. For example, the Christian notion of the *creatio ex nihilo*—that God created the world *out of nothing*—is a notion that cannot be found in the Hebrew Scriptures. But the conviction of God's "undivided sovereignty over nature" can, and both are rooted in the experienced reality of covenant and grace. Exodus interprets beginnings!

EXODUS AND HOPE

The exodus was also the key to understanding the future. The God who by his gracious election had shown his sovereignty over nature and history and had by his words of promise taken Israel up into his love *would be faithful.* Creation is in reality eschatology. The creation stories in Genesis are not really about what happened "back there," but about what can happen up ahead. They are a response to questions about what is possible for humankind and for the world. The recurring theme of the goodness of creation (Gen 1) affirms that the world and humankind are redeemable. It was the very character of God himself that created this redemptive confidence in the future. His dynamic and purposive presence created a forward thrust in Israel's mind. Thus the restlessness and "forward leaning" that has been so much a part of Hebrew history!

It is this "forward leaning" that Jürgen Moltmann believes set the religion of Israel apart from the religions of the Canaanites.[6] For the Canaanite, the holy place—the place where God lived and where he could be found—was the "high place"; for the Hebrew the holy place was the "highway"—the place where God was on the move toward the fulfillment of his promises. The chief characteristic of what Moltmann call "presence theologies," such as that of the Canaanites, is the *possession* of God. The theophany is its own end. To experience the holy and to enjoy it is sufficient unto itself. Such presence religions have no sense of a God in movement toward greater fulfillments to come.

Moltmann suggests that in the self-revelation of Yahweh, there is always a sense of a God *known* but not *possessed,* of a God who gives himself but does so primarily in his promises. As we have already observed, it may be more proper to translate the name Yahweh, given to Moses at the burning bush, as "I will be!" than as "I am." The presence of the Hebrew God is presence with promise.

In conclusion, then, we may say that the exodus unites creation and new creation. Thus the whole span of history is contained, at least in embryo, in the Sinai epiphany.

COVENANT AND LAW

As the Hebrew story is unfolded in the Pentateuch, the exodus presents us with a new phenomenon and a new motif—law! We have seen that the Genesis narratives of creation, flood, and tribal establishment have all been dominated by the notion of the covenant. This involved the implied covenant act of creation with Adam and Eve, the explicit covenant spoken to Noah and including "every creature" that was with him in the ark, and then the covenant of election and promise to Abraham and his sons. Now, with Moses, a new and equally powerful theme enters the Hebrew story. Anyone who is familiar with the history of the Judeo-Christian tradition or with Western culture in general is aware of the importance of moral law, especially as embodied in the Decalogue or Ten Commandments.

How are these two—the covenant tradition and the law tradition—to be understood? What is their relationship to one another, and which is to be decisive—covenant or law—in properly understanding the biblical story? Is it the case that the covenant motif, creative and pregnant with meaning as it has been, was nevertheless a preliminary stage in the unfolding of the meaning of biblical religion? Is it the case that once the law is given, the covenant can recede into the background as the primary way of understanding the relationship of God to his people?

All that has been said above will prepare us for the answer to these questions. Yet the confusion that still persists in both of the great biblically based religions of the West requires a clear answer: *The covenant remains the determinative motif*, and law can only be misunderstood except *within the context of the covenant*. Covenant illuminates law and gives content to law rather than the reverse being true.

TWO TYPES OF RELIGION

For purposes of our study, it is possible to identify two basic types of religion. I suggest that virtually all positive religions—or at least those that offer to the adherent some kind of redemptive or life-enhancing fulfillment—represent either the one or the other of these two types, or else seek in some manner to combine the two. I have attempted to express the cogent difference between these approaches by the following symbols:

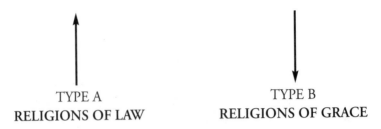

TYPE A
RELIGIONS OF LAW

TYPE B
RELIGIONS OF GRACE

We will designate type A religions as religions of law, or *legalisms.* The distinguishing mark of religions of law, despite their manifold variety and many permutations throughout human history, is the dependence of redemption on *human initiative.* This is the reason for the ascending arrow. In a typical legalism, the divine legislator establishes the criteria according to which favor, fellowship, and blessing can be achieved. God or the gods establish the law, but humankind alone can accomplish it or make it effective. In a legalism, our relationship to God is determined by our fulfilling—often by the *degree* of our fulfilling—the law. We *become* the people of God, achieve his friendship, approval, and favor by our initiative. In a true legalism, if we fall short in our struggle toward legal sufficiency, we remain outside of God's affection, or, in the extreme, we fail to enter into blessedness or salvation. One result of such a view is the emphasis on "rewards and punishment" so common in religions of law.

Is it too much to speculate that most popular religion, regardless of the tradition within which it lives, tends to be legalistic? Even religions that in their more sophisticated forms seek to escape from it often seem unable to do so at the confessional level. To what degree do most popular expressions of Christian faith operate on a rewards and punishment pattern? Perhaps our language betrays us. Which of us has not experienced a moment of unexpected good fortune and remarked with joy, "What have I done to deserve this?" Or, meeting with misfortune, who has not ruefully asked the same question? The assumption in both cases is that our well-being, good fortune, and the divine favor depend on our achievement.

While a religion of grace may well include the concept of law, the role of law is completely different from that in a true legalism. In a religion of grace, the role of law is established by the covenant in which it is given. The meaning of law flows from the meaning of covenant, and the establishment of the covenant is the gracious act of God. The descending arrow makes clear where the initiative lies in a religion of grace: it lies with God. In such a religion, law, whatever its role, is never to be understood as a means of achieving God's favor. Indeed, the law is meaningless except within the covenant.

Even civil law is an expression of covenant. Only citizens of a state or community who voluntarily choose to live within it are considered subject to its laws. Thus I am not bound by the laws of Denmark or subject to the attendance rules of the Rotary Club. Belonging gives rules meaning and power.

A homely example may be helpful. When my younger daughter, Suzii, was six years old, she had a neighborhood playmate named Jenny. Jenny's life, as we could observe it, left a lot to be desired. Her father, a traveling salesman, was rarely at home, and her socially ambitious mother was preoccupied. As a result, the child had little supervision. When she came home from first-grade classes, she would frequently be alone until late in the evening. As a consequence, she was able to wander the neighborhood at will. My daughter, who sometimes vexed under family rules and regulations, envied Jenny's freedom. For instance, our children were under strict orders to report to us at home when darkness fell. Jenny would often be playing under the streetlight until nine or even ten.

One hot summer night at midnight I went into the yard to turn off a lawn sprinkler and spied Jenny sitting in the children's swing set in our backyard looking wistfully into our lighted den. When I called her name, I startled her so that she fell backward to the ground in a cloud of dust. I rushed to her and found her unhurt. She explained her presence: "Nobody's at home at my house." And nobody was!

Now let us suppose that Jenny, weary of loneliness, decided she wanted to join the Christian clan, with all of its commotion and laughter and tears. And let us suppose that, having learned from our Suzii what the family rules were, she made an earnest effort to fulfill them. She even made sure every evening to be at home when darkness fell. Then suppose one day she confronted me with the following proposition: "I have kept all the laws of the Christian family and have earned my right to be your child. I am now one of you." What would be my response? Would I not have to say, "I'm sorry, Jenny, it doesn't work that way. Those rules have no bearing on you. You cannot climb the ladder of law to family membership."

Indeed, the only way in which she could enter into the community of our family, given the right legal circumstances, would be by an adoption in which the initiative would lie with my wife and me. If by our gracious act she were to be so included, then I could say to her, "Jenny, you are now one of our own! You are as much our child as Suzii or Anne or Bobby or David, as much ours as if we had given you birth. Welcome to our hearthstone and to our love. And by the way," I would then add, "you are to be in the house tonight when it gets dark!"

LEGALISM AND GRACE

It is, then, the gracious act of God that constitutes community and membership in it. It will be our contention that Hebrew faith at its best and Christian faith at its best are both rooted in the twin traditions of covenant and grace. We will also argue that the Decalogue—the Ten Commandments—can only be adequately understood as a religion of grace.

The use of such a term as the "moral law" to refer to the Ten Commandments is in itself problematic. To call the Decalogue the moral law is to obscure the powerful word of grace it contains. Even the designation "Ten Commandments"—a name we can scarcely avoid—has the sound of legalism. This has helped to popularize in Christian circles a sharp and unjust distinction between Old Testament and New Testament religion. The use of the term "law" to describe the Ten Commandments may lend support to a view I often heard in Christian churches during my youth. I was told that Hebrew religion was a religion of law and Christian religion was religion of grace. As Walter Harrelson put it, "Along with the term *Old* we have inherited another venerable and mischief-working distinction: the Old Testament has been identified as the book of the law in contrast to the New Testament, the Christian book of grace and free forgiveness."[7] Nothing links these two biblically-derived religions more faithfully or more fruitfully than this fact: at bottom they are both rooted in the covenant God and are thus religions of grace.

This does not mean, of course, that either faith has always or even often been free of the tendency to introduce elements of legalism. "Every religion," adds Harrelson, "can be turned into an unwholesome legalism."[8] But if it is so that biblical religion is essentially a religion of grace, why has it been so haunted by the specter of legalism?

THE PERSISTENCE OF LEGALISM

Part of the answer to the question posed above has to do with the relative ease of fulfillment offered by legalism. A legal understanding of faith and ethics seems to afford us with a clear and simple access to religious security, particularly when held in common with a superficial understanding of sin. Legalism without a profound sense of inwardness seems to resolve all moral issues into concrete rules of behavior. Such rules may be rigorous and demanding, but they are possible to fulfill. The negative language in which "laws" are usually cast tends to conceal their optimistic assessment of human nature. One does not bother to prohibit what cannot be avoided. "Thou shalt not" implies "Thou canst!" Behind the stern language in which legalism is often expressed is the kind of simple optimism described in the previous chapter.

But shallow optimism is not the only reason for the persistence of legalism in the synagogue and in the church. Legalism may be a caricature of biblical faith, but caricatures are not meaningless; they reflect reality even as they distort it. Not even a distortion of the truth is totally without truth. Legalism must be a response to something in the soul of the believer, something that requires we take it seriously. What is the religious instinct behind legalism?

I frequently tell my students that any idea or attitude or doctrine that has been held tenaciously by a significant number of people for a significant period of time probably contains a valid insight or has a valid experience behind it. The depth and persistence of legalism is perhaps rooted in the longing for norms for the control of life. The longing for norms reflects the uniquely human moral sense and the related terror of decision. How does one decide and act in a world that confronts us all with the responsibility of being moral?

The need for credible and durable norms is probably a universal need. We have suggested above that norms arise from life in community. If this is so, perhaps we can understand the moral crisis that seems to be so deeply felt in Western society today. One of the characteristics of American society in particular is the collapse of the structures that made for community in the past. Many of the forces at work in the dynamic and mobile society of the West work against a sense of stability.

These same forces often operate as a powerful solvent of all moral criteria. Where the breakdown of community is most advanced, the longing for stabilizing rules of order and decision may become intense. Therefore it is easy to understand the longing for trustworthy norms to guide the decisions of life. It is also easy to understand why biblical religion has so persistently yielded to legalism and why the commandments have so commonly been read as a law code. But what are the shortcomings of legalism?

THE COST OF LEGALISM

One of the attractions of legalism is its apparent simplicity and directness of application. Amid moral uncertainty, it is bracing to hear a clear-cut command, "Thou shalt" or "Thou shalt not." The longing for moral absolutes becomes intense when the sense of right and wrong threatens to be buried under the weight of a thousand qualifications. But in practice, the search for moral absolutes is often deceptive, and concrete counsel may prove elusive and confusing. Why?

The problem lies in the "positiveness" of the law or in what Harrelson calls its "absolutism."[9] It can't deal with the complexity of life. This complexity is often revealed in the conflict that can arise between the commandments themselves. What are we to do when the law urges us to seek justice but also to love mercy? More often we discover the complexity of decision when we realize the great numbers of people to whom we relate and whose lives are affected by our actions and decisions. A rule that is clear and unambiguous when only one person is involved may give little guidance where the interests and needs of many people are in question.

Many of the most difficult moral issues are difficult precisely because of these complexities—that is, the complexity of life but also the complexity of the law itself. When we face real decisions involving the lives of people, such absolute rules may provide little moral comfort. This is why a consistent legalism has been called an ethic for the mountaintops that ignores the foothills in which we actually live.

Many of our most agonizing moral dilemmas arise from the difficulties that confront us when we attempt to apply absolute rules to the ambiguities of the human situation. How does one apply the commandment against killing in a situation in which the preservation of one life puts into jeopardy the life of someone else? An example would be the case of an abortion in which the physician must put at risk the life either of the mother or the fetus. Or how does one apply the rule when the protection of the life and well-being of an individual, a family, or, in the case of war, of a society or nation appears to necessitate the killing of others?

It seems to be possible for some people, when faced with the complex situations of life, to take refuge in an ethical absolutism. It is possible, for instance, to hold to a type of pacifism that refuses to inflict death under any circumstance. If the alternative to killing another is to be killed, then we might be willing to admire such a refusal as heroic consistency. If, on the other hand, the refusal to kill were to result in the death of others, and especially of the innocent, it might be harder for us to offer approval. Surely there are cases where ethical consistency and legal absolutism might seem less than noble and more like what Paul Lehmann calls "a failure of nerve."[10] How do we respond when the applying of the "letter of the law "might cause unnecessary human suffering? Is it ever the case that the demands of human compassion require us to qualify and perhaps modify the absolute demands of the law?

Because of the difficulty of applying the law in any unqualified way in the manifold situations of living, legalism has always tended to dissolve into complex systems of rules and regulations for the control of society. Such a system or rules is called a "casuistry." This means an elaboration of general rules and principles into cases and subcases for application to specific situations. Such systems of concrete law, as we see for example in the holiness codes of Leviticus and in far more detailed form in the Talmudic law codes of later Israel, are an attempt to bring the law down from the mountaintop and apply it to situations that don't seem to allow moral absolutism. They are attempts to tell us how we should behave when faced with decisions that don't yield to moral simplicities. They seek to give guidance where the demands of justice and love seem to collide and where love of family, neighbor, and nation intersect.

It is easy to ridicule the outlandish systems of rules and regulations that sometimes result from the attempt to apply moral absolutes to real human needs. Systems of positive law, with their cases, subcases, and exceptions, sometimes lend themselves to caricature. But we should not forget that behind these "casuistries" of law lies the earnest longing for trustworthy norms in the face of moral decision. The casuistries arise out of an effort to give people moral guidance when the practical situation does not allow the luxury of doing the ideal thing.

Every such system that allows us to qualify the absoluteness of the law arises out of the urgency of the law. We recognize its seriousness. We hear the moral demand of its "thou shalt" or "thou shalt not." And because we take the ideal seriously—"Thou shalt not kill; Thou shalt not commit adultery; Thou shalt not steal"—we talk endlessly about how we can best serve that ideal in a less-than-ideal world. Behind every debate over euthanasia or just war is the shadow of the law.

THE COVENANT AS GRACE

Of course, the covenant stands above and gives meaning to the law. However we may think of the law and especially the Decalogue, we must not think that it creates fellowship and life, either with God or with each other. The instincts of legalism—that life needs norms for deciding—are not wrong. But they are replete with the potential for evil when the law is taken out of its context or given priority over covenant. *Law has no meaning except within covenant.* The priority of the covenant over the law is nowhere better expressed than in the preface to the Decalogue in Exodus 20:1. This brief but crucial prologue to the

Ten Commandments is usually omitted when they are read publicly or when they are framed and posted in church or home. Thus the Decalogue is cast in its common "apodictic" (absolutist) light: "Thou shalt" and "Thou shalt not."

But the preface in Exodus 20:1 puts the commandments in the context of the Covenant God. The basis of the newly constituted (or reconstituted) people of Israel is not their worthy character but the free unmerited act of God—not "Thou shalt" but "I am the Lord your God." God does not make the covenant a conditional affair dependent on the fulfillment of the law; it is presented by Moses, to use the modern jargon, as "a done deal."

The law has come into being because of this accomplished fact—that God has made them his people. This fact is based purely on the initiative of God. Yahweh has brought forth the slaves to freedom, and therefore he is in a position to lay on them the responsibilities inherent in the covenant community and expressed in the Decalogue. As Harrelson puts it, "God's mercy precedes his laying down of the covenant requirements; the Decalogue arises in a context of grace."[12] More than this, the law shows forth the character of the gracious God and the kind of relationship this God seeks with his people. Karl Barth follows the reformers when he reminds us that law is the *form* of the gospel. That is, it shows us the concrete shape that a living community of love for God and for one another will take. So once again we end up repeating our formula: *community and covenant are the context for law.*

COVENANT AND RESPONSIBILITY

We have said that the law is meaningful only in the context of the covenant brought into being by God's gracious election. But this act of grace creates a new context for and reason for the law. It creates a people trusting in God and in one another, and this means responsibility. We sometimes overlook the obvious fact that the word *responsibility* has to do with the *ability* to *respond* and that this requires an existing situation of community. Whenever I take the initiative in friendship or love, the result is a new fact of human mutuality. I call forth from the other a response, and response-ability is born. This is the other side of the divine initiative, and it becomes a second frame-of-reference for understanding the law. The key to interpreting the Decalogue is, in Lehmann's words, "responsible reciprocity."[13]

Thus the question for me when I am confronted with the commandment "Thou shalt not steal," or "Thou shalt have no other gods before me," is not one of *obedience* but of *response.* I should not ask, "How do I obey this law?"

but "How does this commandment provide me with guidance in living and enriching the relationship to neighbor and to God?" So the covenant-making God and the covenant-made community determine the concrete character of my response.

In the beginning, all moral behavior springs from gratitude and love toward God. Then of necessity it overflows in action toward my covenant neighbor. I do not *obey* God; I *respond* to him and to his gracious act. I don't merely "do my duty" to my neighbor, nor am I content to treat him with *legal* propriety. I act *toward* him as we two are mutually bound together by grace. This mutual responsibility—toward God and toward *each* other—will provide the fundamental structure of the Decalogue.

This is what Lehmann meant when he said that the commandments are *descriptive* rather than *prescriptive*.[14] That is, they do not legislate action but *describe* human life as it is intended to be under God. Or, as Harrelson puts it, "These are not laws in the ordinary sense of law. The Ten Commandments are much more akin to statements about the character of life in community."[15]

If all of this is so, then we can begin to understand why the Ten Commandments are guaranteed to become either irrelevant or arbitrary when they are separated from an awareness of the covenant God and when they lack a joyful sense of grace. We suggested above that our understanding of God shapes dynamically our life in the world in all its aspects. This surely applies to the Decalogue. Israel's encounter with the maker of covenants gave rise to the law. So the key to interpreting the commandments is for us to allow what we have learned about God—in creation, in grace, and in covenant—to open our eyes and our hearts to their meaning.

RESPONSIBILITY AND FREEDOM

God's act in creating a community of love and grace provides us with the means of answering one of the most troubling and persistent questions in Christian theology: the question of divine sovereignty and human freedom. In the previous chapter we described the God of Hebrew faith as sovereign and therefore in control of the world and of the events of history. This sovereignty meant God could be trusted and that his promises would be fulfilled. But it is easy to misunderstand the nature of God's sovereignty in the world as some kind of all-embracing determinism. But God's act in bestowing on us community—both with himself and with our covenant fellows—puts down decisively any theology of divine determinism. Responsibility means the ability to respond, and this is meaningless without freedom.

Confusing God's creative sovereignty and God's election of Israel with some kind of metaphysical determinism is a distortion of the Old Testament faith. The only irresistible divine predestination is his character as creative love. Insofar as God is grace, then grace is most certainly irresistible. The old hyper-Calvinist is right about this! It is quite impossible for God to be otherwise than what he is or for his dealings with his creatures to be untouched by his grace. But his grace does not imprison his people in a bondage of obligation. This is *not* the character of grace! Rather, grace is that which stretches out the horizons of responsible selfhood. Grace does not mean slavery; grace means freedom.

Despite their willingness to speak of God as foreknowing Jacob's destiny and directing the paths of Joseph, the Hebrews were never "Calvinists." How could they be, when their very existence came about in a call to *responsible* reciprocity? Notice once again how responsibility points to freedom. We are called by the act of God and the presence of the neighbor to *respond*. And the call to respond means the *ability* to do so. Responsibility without *ability* is meaningless.

The Hebrew took for granted that he stood before God and the world in freedom. This did not mean, as it does in some expressions of Christian doctrine, a mere *psychological* freedom. According to such a notion, I might *feel* free—that is, I might feel myself to be free of external restraints—while I yet acknowledge the divine determination of my every thought and deed. But this is not what the Hebrew meant. Hebrew freedom was real, metaphysical freedom, the freedom by which one could shape one's own destiny and even change the destiny of the world and of God.

But the Hebrew assumption of real freedom did not rest on a carefully thought-out philosophy of nature and God; once again, it rested on the call of God to *response* and to *responsibility*. Without freedom, any so-called response is a pretense—it is at best God responding to himself through us. Without freedom, responsibility is a contradiction in terms.

Not only did the call into God's grace and covenant fellowship make freedom necessary; it made it real! Being in community did not restrict; it liberated. The law did not enslave; it set one free! As the Hebrew saw it, the law only became oppressive and the enemy of self-actualization when it was taken out of its covenant context. We will argue that the basis for being human rests on the possibilities created by a healthy response to God and to neighbor. The commandments do not suppress; they liberate. They are instruments of freedom.

ELECTION AND OBEDIENCE

We will consider shortly another aspect of the question of grace and freedom. But a different question now engages us: Did Israel's election depend on her moral superiority or goodness? More important for understanding the law, did her continuation as God's people depend on her faithfulness? What would happen if she failed to keep the law? If the covenant and the law rested on God's initiative, on his gracious choosing, did its continuing depend on the faithfulness of Israel?

It is significant that the Decalogue carries with it no threats or catalog of penalties. It does not speak in conditional terms: "*If* Israel will keep my laws *then* she will by my people." The absence of condition or threat supports Lehmann's contention that the Decalogue is descriptive and not prescriptive. What bearing did the faithfulness of Israel have on the purposes of God for his people? Could Israel's disobedience bring it to disaster?

Israel herself was far from clear or unanimous on the matter. If the commandments themselves were free from penalties or curses, the Hebrew law that developed from them was not. The elaborations of the law in the Levitical code are replete with warnings and punishments. And the liturgy of covenant renewal described in the Deuteronomic literature provided, with ceremonial punctuation, the curses and blessings the Decalogue lacks. Furthermore, the prophets were often emphatic about the threat of divine retaliation and even rejection that awaited a faithless Israel. Thus the theme of divine faithfulness expressed in the patriarchal narratives and in the exodus drama was often called into question by the fact of Israel's apostasy and sin.

Did their election depend on their obedience? Commentators today are not in agreement, although a certain degree of consensus seems to exist. Ronald Clements asserts that the covenant, though instituted by God, depended for its continuance on Israel's obedience.[16] Nahum Sarna, on the other hand, sees the covenant as binding Israel to God unilaterally and unequivocally. He writes, "The Bible describes . . . nothing less than the assertion of the conclusion of an eternally binding pact between God and his people."[17]

Johnstone agrees with Sarna that the covenant in the final analysis is not dependent on Israel's obedience. He anchors his opinion in the history of their subsequent failure and renewal. Israel's own story is the awesome proof of the divine grace. Her recalcitrance and sin could certainly break the divine heart, but it could not in the end devastate the redemptive community. God's faithfulness would triumph through renewal. Grace was not determinative but restorative and redemptive. Johnstone writes that, after failure, "the covenant is nonetheless remade on the identical terms as before to declare that though all men should be false yet he will remain faithful. The covenant unilaterally abrogated by man is unilaterally reinstated by God."[18]

Put in the light of failure and redemption, Clements in the last analysis seems to agree with Nahum and Johnstone, for he takes seriously Hosea's announcement that Israel's harlotry has been forgiven by the steadfast love of God. "Hosea is here asserting," he writes, "that Yahweh's judgment would not be the end of Israel, since the covenant was founded on the divine love, and that love would persevere."[19] So also Lester Meyer, according to whom judgment is real but mercy is forever.[20]

In conclusion, it seems evident that despite the sense of responsibility to the law and to the God who gives it, and despite the moral outrage expressed by the prophets against the nation's unfaithfulness, there was a steady movement toward a deeper sense of grace in Israel. God demanded her obedience, but her disobedience was not the death of the covenant. And the more desperate her national and moral condition became, the more the prophets seem to trust in the steadfastness of God. The counterpoint of failure and promise in Amos, Hosea, Isaiah, Jeremiah, Ezekiel, and Deutero-Isaiah led to a deeper sense that Israel's destiny finally rested not on her obedience but on the faithfulness of God.

The ability of the great prophets to look beyond the bleakness of Israel's eighth-century situation rests on this vision of grace. The glowing canvases of hope and universal redemption that we find in Hosea, in Isaiah's "peaceable kingdom," in Jeremiah's announcement of a New Covenant, and in Deutero-Isaiah's promise of a New Exodus—all of these represent the birth of an eschatology of hope beyond failure. That eschatology rested firmly on a theology of covenant grace. Past promises and the exodus epiphany, and the ensuing mercies and restorations became the basis of confidence in that future. The future hope of Israel was created in the hearts of the prophets out of the content of epiphany and promise.

GRACE AND FREEDOM

We argued above that a theology of grace such as we have described is the opposite of determinism. Surely some of my readers will respond to this notion with raised eyebrows. Is it not a paradox at best, or a contradiction at worst, to suggest that Israel's covenant destiny would be fulfilled despite her failure to become what God intended? Would not a sure and certain fulfillment of that destiny be fatal to any meaningful sense of freedom or moral responsibility? If one is to be worthy of salvation, is it not also necessary to be able to be worthy of rejection and judgment? Weren't the Calvinists of old right when they declared that irresistible grace and complete predestination were one? Was it the Methodist theologian Edwin Lewis who insisted, in the interest of moral freedom, that "A fellow has to be able to get damned around here"?

Once again we are brought back willy-nilly to the question we addressed above: free will and determinism. This debate that once was essentially a theological or philosophical one has now been immeasurably widened in scope by developments in the special sciences, such as biology, psychology, and physics. But quite apart from the conflict of modern libertarian humanism and behavioristic psychology, the debate continues in religious discussion and dialogue.

We asked above if God's omnipotence and omniscience precluded human freedom and moral responsibility. Now we must ask whether a theology of grace does the same thing. Or does this notion rest on a misunderstanding? Most debates about free will or determinism (or its theological equivalent, predestination) begin with a false assumption: that we must espouse either a complete determinism or an absolute freedom. But both of these notions, when considered carefully, prove to be meaningless and, if they are taken seriously, they tend to collapse into one another.

Consider the notion of absolute freedom. Those who argue for such a dogma suggest that if freedom is infringed even in the smallest degree it is effectively denied. Freedom must be absolute or it ceases to be freedom. If, for example, I am the person I am and if my choices and actions are shaped by my inherited chemistry and biology, my past history and that of my family, then I am no longer meaningfully free. I am enclosed in a destiny that precludes freedom. The social and biological determinism of a growing number of my students reflects this despair of freedom, and I find in many of them a resulting sense of moral helplessness and resignation.

But the emptiness of the notion of absolute freedom is revealed by the way in which it tends to slip into its opposite. Our language betrays us! Suppose I were to lay down my pen (or forsake my computer) and assault the person in the next room. If I were then asked why I had done this thing, I would be unlikely to answer, "Because I was free!" I would not argue that as a wholly free person this action was as open to me as any other. Would I not rather say, "I don't know! Something *got into* me," or "Something *came over* me," or perhaps. "I wasn't *myself!* I felt this urge!" Are these phrases the language of freedom or of compulsion? And I would likely deny any moral responsibility for an action that was not my free choice.

The notion of absolute freedom implies unlimited possibilities and unlimited choices. But in actual experience, to have unlimited choices is to have no real choices at all. There is no real freedom except in a limiting and creative context. If I am given a million options I am paralyzed; if I am give a dozen I can decide and I can act. The biblical notion of election will not be confused with determination or detailed predestination if it is remembered that God's election of Israel was an election *to community*. The law gave concreteness and possibility to their life in community. It provided the *context* for decision, but the decision remained that of each Hebrew.

Freedom in grace is real but it can never be absolute. Indeed, freedom was real for Israel *because* it was not absolute. Grace liberated because it never left them unsupported in a sea of indeterminacy. It never abandoned them to their feeble powers to shape life and give it meaning. Above all, it never gave them over to blind fate.

My second daughter—a child who was not in times past unfamiliar with the urge to rebellion—spoke to me recently about her adolescent years. "You and Mother let us grow up," she said, "and make our own decisions and our own mistakes, but I always knew that you were there *for me*. So," she added, "I was never really afraid to risk learning and trying to be who and what I might be." What she was saying, I think, was that she knew she could be many things, but she could never escape from our overshadowing love. This was the absolute that opened the way for wisdom and folly, joy and sorrow, self-actualization and self-diminution, justice and injustice, fulfillment and disappointment, but all within the persistence of our love.

THE FUNCTIONS OF THE LAW

We have observed that the laws of the Decalogue carry no "curses" or "blessings" and, with the possible exception of the fourth commandment, do not deal with consequences. We have also argued that Israel's inclusion in Yahweh's covenant was not a consequence of their obedience. We have even suggested that failure to fulfill the law did not mean divine rejection. What then was the function of the law?

I recall as a lad reading the words of the psalmist describing those whose "delight is in the law of the LORD" (Ps 1:2). I can also recall a feeling of amazement and distress at this confession. Was I really expected to *delight* in the law? I might view it with awe and respect; I might grudgingly admire its majesty and admit its value for my growth and discipline, but why would the psalmist view it with delight? His sense of joy in the law suggests that he understood it in a context other than that of legalism; he understood it in the context of grace. Once again we are reminded that law has no meaning except within the covenant.

But within the covenant it was rich with meaning. As we have seen, the law was not an arbitrary imposition upon the covenant but, in Clements's words, "an expression of the grace in which Yahweh had brought Israel out of Egypt and had taken them to be his people."[21] It was the summation of the character of God himself. And its existence facilitated the Hebrews' deepening relation to God and to each other. In other words, the law gave a concrete framework for *response-ability* to God and to neighbor. The law can be seen to function at two complementary levels: (1) the individual's relation to God and (2) to his or her covenant fellows:

(1) *The law as the preserver of covenant.* The law was not a means of securing covenant, but it was a means for actualizing the covenant community and of bringing it to its fullest possibilities. The violation of God's law is not only an affront to grace, it is, as Sarna puts it, "a breach . . . that undermines society."[22] Indeed, "the welfare of society, the integrity of its fabric, is contingent upon the observance of the law."

(2) *The law as response to grace.* The delight of the psalmist puts the law directly into the context of community. It seems to have served the member of that community in three interdependent ways:

(a) *As a mark of belonging.* Even when the Hebrews vexed under its demands, the very existence of the law was a continuing reminder that they were embraced by God, much as the protective and sometimes restrictive structure of parental care is a reminder of inclusion. I can recall times as an adolescent when I took refuge from temptation in the rules imposed on me by parents. More than once I opted out of risky or questionable proposals by appealing to the law. "I'd really like to, guys," I might say, "but my dad would kill me!" Behind my mild hypocrisy, I was comforted to know that there were those who cared sufficiently about me to provide guidance and impose norms. So it was with the Hebrew: "I am God's! I belong to his people. How do I know? I have his law!"

(b) *As a measuring rod for growth.* My own negative response to law is in part an inheritance from Luther and his thoroughgoing theology of grace. So vigorous was his reaction against the shallow commercialism and legalism of late Catholic Medieval theology that he appeared at times to deny any positive role to the law. He could not deny that it was holy because it was from God, but he understood its sole religious function to be that of the "schoolmaster" who brings the sinner to confession and to grace. He was reluctant to speak of a function of the law in the life of faith.

But this is not the whole of the story, for the central place given to the Decalogue in Luther's catechism makes clear that he understood its positive function in grace. Part of this function is providing a standard to guide the steps of the maturing member of the covenant.

My wife and I recently undertook the remodeling of the den in our home. Before the painting began, I made a careful examination of the woodwork. On one of the door facings I discovered something that gave me a moment of regret: a faint but discernible series of marks ascending the doorpost. To each mark was appended an initial and a date, for instance, "A. 11/61; B. 4/67; S. 4/70." Near the top, the undated marks M and D clearly designated Mom and Dad. You could watch the growth of Anne, Bob, Suzii, and finally David as they measured themselves against the fullness of maturity. (Never mind that Bob's last entry towered over Dad's!) In a similar way, the law served as a reminder of the possibilities that still remained to be realized. So the law for the Hebrew was a challenge for growth because it was a reliable reminder of the fullness of God.

(c) *As a concrete means for gratitude,* for giving back to God his manifest goodness and grace. Gratitude is the most positive and creative force behind obedience. This is evident to any child who has ever followed the admonition of a parent, not out of fear, but out of love. Gratitude for inclusion in God's grace is the true dynamic and the inner spirit of the law. We will suggest below that gratitude toward God opens the heart to the neighbor and provides the link between the two "tables" of the Decalogue.

My astonishment at the delight with which the psalmist viewed the law would have been allayed if, as a youth I had read his words more carefully. Then perhaps I would have caught his true spirit. I would have discovered how deeply the love of the law was rooted in the grace and faithfulness of God: "You are righteous, O LORD, and your judgments are right . . . . Your promise is well tried and your servant loves it" (Ps 119:137, 140).

Trustworthy, promises, love—these are the world of covenant that give the law its meaning.

NOTES

[1] H. Richard Niebuhr, *The Meaning of Revelation* (New York: Collier Books, Macmillan Publishing Company, 1960), 68-69.

[2] R. E. Clements, *Prophesy and Covenant* (Napierville IL: Alec R. Allenson, Inc., 1965).

[3] Nahum Sarna, *Exploring Exodus: The Heritage of Biblical Faith* (Napierville IL: Alec R. Allenson, Inc., 1965), 137.

[4] Ibid.

[5] Friedrich Schleiermacher, *The Christian Faith,* trans. and ed., H. R. Mackintosh and J. S. Stewart (Philadelphia: Fortress Press, 1976), #36, para. 1, 142-43.

[6] Jürgen Moltmann, *Theology of Hope* (New York and Evanston: Harper and Row, Publishers, 1965), 95-106.

[7] Walter Harrelson, *The Ten Commandments and Human Rights* (Philadelphia: Fortress Press, 1980), 5.

[8] Ibid.

[9] Ibid.

[10] Paul Lehmann, *The Decalogue and a Human Future* (Grand Rapids: Wm. B. Eerdmans Publishing Company, 1995).

[11] Joseph Fletcher, *Situaion Ethics: The New Morality* (Philadelphia: Westminster Press, 1965), 69f.

[12] Harrelson, *Ten Commandments and Human Rights,* 46.

[13] Paul Lehmann, *The Decalogue and a Human Future* , 17.

[14] Ibid., 22.

[15] Harrelson, *The Ten Commandments and Human Rights,* 15.

[16] Clements, *Prophesy and Covenant,* 71.

[17] Sarna, *Exploring Exodus.*

[18] W. Johnstone, *Exodus* (Sheffield England: JSOT Press, 1990), 52.

[19] Clements, *Prophesy and Covenant,* 111.

[20] Lester Meyer, *The Message of Exodus* (Minneapolis: Augsburg Publishing House, 1983), 123.

[21] Clements, *Prophesy and Covenant,* 110.

[22] Sarna, *Exploring Exodus,* 143.

~

Chapter Five

The Ten Commandments:
Their Origins, Character, and Scope

This brief study is not the place for what the scholar would call a "diachronic" examination, that is, a study "through time," seeking to determine with exactness each step in the development of the Hebrew law tradition. We will not address in detail the process by which the present texts of the Pentateuch in general or of the Ten Commandments or Decalogue in particular were forged during the centuries of Hebrew history. Our declared purpose is more "synchronic"; that is, we are concerned with understanding the law as it came to be the heart of the Hebrew's story of covenant. However, brief remarks concerning the origins of the law and its relation to the traditions of Israel's neighbors will be useful.

ORIGINS AND ANTECEDENTS

(1) *Antecedents for law and covenant.* As we have seen, the practice of covenant- or treaty-making was apparently of great antiquity in the Near East. Archeological investigation has revealed numerous examples of covenant-making among such predecessors and contemporaries of the Hebrews as the Hittites of Asia Minor, the Egyptians, and the Akkadians of the Fertile Crescent. It also seems

likely that the Sinai covenant and the Decalogue, as the expression of that covenant, owe not a little to these models.

We also distinguished between covenants of mutuality, or "parity covenants," in which the contracting parties are equals, and "suzerainty covenants," which are bestowed by a lord or other figure of authority on those embraced by them. We found the closest analogy to the Sinai covenant in the suzerainty-vassal type. But to suggest that such models lie behind the form of the Hebrew covenant is in no way to deny its originality or to suggest that its meaning can be reduced to the sum-total of Hittite or Akkadian models. We will need to comment more fully on the differences between the two.

(2) *Moses and the origins of the Decalogue.* At what point and under what circumstances did the commandments begin? It seems clear that they are set forth in the biblical story as the basic expression of the covenant of Yahweh with his people. But this does not tell us whether that understanding goes back to Sinai and the wilderness or whether it represents Israel's gradual interpretation of her national experience throughout the centuries. And the occasional restatement and reformulations of the law in the Hebrew Scriptures remind us that the Decalogue has a history. Still, the elaboration and expansion that the legal tradition undergoes in the Levitical and Deuteronomic literature make clear the importance the Decalogue had for shaping their subsequent history.

The question of the origin of the law is made more difficult by growing doubts in some scholarly circles that the Hebrew nation truly had its beginning in an exodus from Egypt. For instance, scholars like Gottwald and Cheney have sought to trace the origins of Hebrew nationality to an uprising of peasants in the land of Canaan against their Canaanite overlords.[1] Some commentators have also wondered whether the sophistication of the covenant code in Exodus did not require a later date and a more complex social experience than the exodus narrative provides. Some scholars have found the origin of the Decalogue in the cultic practices described in later Hebrew society, and others have suggested a much later seventh century BC beginning in the reforms of Josiah described in 2 Kings 22 and 23.

The matter is not a critical one for our purposes, but it is interesting that there seems to be among contemporary commentators a movement back to an early date for the commandments, at least in their simplest form. This is due in part to a growing skepticism about the simplistic application of evolutionary thinking to the interpretation of past cultures. That is, it is no longer assumed that earlier means more primitive and that subtlety and theological sophistication always represent a later, more mature phase in cultural development.

The question of Moses as author and lawgiver cannot, of course, be answered definitively, but there is some feeling today that a Mosaic origin is at least as plausible as any of the proposed alternatives. Walter Harrelson's conclusions are certainly in keeping with the story as the Hebrews recount it and will serve us as a working hypotheses:

> When we examine the contents [of the Decalogue,] we can see that there is no objection in principle to attributing them to the time of Moses. If it be supposed, as I believe, that Moses did bring a band (perhaps a small band) of slaves from servitude in Egypt, guided them throughout the wilderness for some years, and worked out with them a set of guidelines for their existence resting basically on the exclusive claim of the God who had delivered them from slavery upon the whole of their lives, then the contents of the commandments, although striking, are certainly in keeping with such an understanding of God.[2]

At the very least, we can suspect that in its present form the Decalogue is a reasonable expression of the exodus encounter and response.

THE UNIQUENESS OF THE COVENANT

In biblical faith, God always does his work in the real world of nature and of human beings. This is the deepest meaning of the Christian notion of incarnation and of the church's century-old struggle against docetism. Docetism was a teaching that was rejected by the mainstream of early Christianity. The name derives from a Greek root that means "to seem" or "to appear." True docetists rejected the belief that God was truly incarnate in Jesus. For the docetist, God only seemed to take on human flesh, since the material world was fallen and therefore evil in nature. This meant that it was not possible for the divine to act or to be concretely present in corrupt flesh. *Finitus non capax infinitum*: "The finite is not capable of the infinite!" Thus God cannot have flesh, nor can he have a history.

But in biblical faith, the finite *is* capable of the infinite; God can and does act in the world and every revelation and every act of God has a context and an ancestry. Once God's action has come into the world and has become known, it changes the world and henceforth has a history. Every miracle touches flesh and blood and becomes naturalized. Accordingly, every epiphany is quickly clothed with the swaddling clothes of human culture, language, and ideas.

It should not surprise us that the Sinai covenant resembles in so many ways the covenants that dot the history of the ancient Near East. The test of an epiphany is in its power to transform. So many features of the covenant and the Decalogue are echoed in the traditions of their time. The fact that the Hebrew covenant and their law resemble in important ways those of their neighbors is not of great significance. The significance lies more in the way that, taken as a whole, Israel transformed these older models. The Hebrew covenant is no slavish imitation of Hittite, Akkadian, or Egyptian models. Nahum Sarna has suggested four elements of the Sinai covenant and its attendant code that could be called revolutionary:[3]

(1) *The covenant is between God and the entire people.* Sarna insists that there is no known parallel in history for such an idea. In Hittite parity treaties God is often portrayed as an interested bystander, who, as in the case of Jacob and Laban at Mizpah, is invoked as a witness to the agreement between the parties to the treaty. But in the Sinai covenant he is not bystander; he is party to the agreement and is in fact the *initiating* party. But also unlike the suzerainty treaties imposed by a sovereign on his people, Yahweh's people are not merely vassals; they are full and reciprocal partners and participants with him.

(2) *It is set in a narrative context,* a context from which it cannot be separated. As we have repeatedly asserted, law is meaningless apart from covenant, and the Hebrew covenant is meaningless apart from the drama of burning bush and Sea of Reeds and smoke on the mountain. This is both its origin and its reason for being. It is the story that explains covenant and law, and it is the covenant that will shape Israel's subsequent story.

(3) *It is addressed to the internal as well as the external dimensions of life under God.* As Sarna tells us,

> Near Eastern treaties, being political documents that order interstate relationships, are usually concerned solely with matters of external affairs and ignore internal affairs, except insofar as these might impinge upon the interest of the suzerain state. At Sinai, however, every aspect of the internal life of the "vassal" Israel, particularly interpersonal relationships, falls within the scope of the covenant stipulation.[4]

In other words, if a suzerainty contract established by a lord has as its intent to control and regulate a vassal or a vassal people, then the main concern is conduct rather than attitude. But if in fact the contract has as its purpose the creation of community, and if the hoped-for result is a relationship of "responsive reciprocity" between the parties, then everything that is creative of or destructive of community is its concern. Overt conduct and inward attitude are both matters of supreme importance. Control can live with performance, but community embraces and requires the whole of life—action and attitude, outwardness and inwardness.

The language of the Decalogue itself suggests that not merely the nation is the responsive partner of God. The commandments are directed to the citizens or members of the nation. The "you" addressed in the particular commandment is first person singular and "I am the Lord, *your* God," is the preface to the covenant and the law.

(4) *The Decalogue, while it arises from a concrete history and is set within the community of a specific people, is not "time bound."* Sarna writes, "The terms of the Near East Treaties are invariably time bound rules of mutual conduct pertinent to a specific situation. The Ten Commandments, on the other hand, are general precepts of universal applicability unconditioned by temporal considerations . . . they are of truly binding validity for the present and the future."[5]

But is this so? Whether we must understand the commandments as limited to the context of the community of Israel is crucial to the question of their meaning and relevance to our lives in the world today. Whether Sarna's conclusion is a trustworthy one we will have to consider presently.

THE CHARACTER OF THE DECALOGUE

Not all orderings of the commandments are the same. In the Catholic tradition—a tradition followed by Luther as well—the subdivision of the Decalogue varies from that commonly followed in the Protestant world, although the count remains at ten in each case. In the Catholic arrangement, the first commandments—those concerning monotheism and idolatry—are treated as a single commandment, and the commandment concerning coveting is subdivided. The content is the same in either case. We will follow the Protestant arrangement.

A cursory examination of the commandments makes several facts obvious.

(1) *Their brevity.* Even in the case of commandments with some elaboration, such as the prohibition against idols, against taking God's name in vain, against

dishonor of parents, and against covetousness, the elaboration is minimal. And if we accept Harrelson's judgment, even these elaborations are misleading. Harrelson concludes that these are later additions and that we would approach more nearly the original form if we were to remove even these scant explanatory phrases. Compared with the elaborations of the rules and regulations in the Levitical code, they are succinct to the point of being laconic.

(2) *The negativity of their form.* Only the fourth and fifth commandments, as they now stand, are in a positive form—"Remember to keep the Sabbath Holy" and "Honor father and mother." It is possible—perhaps probable—that these two also were originally cast in the negative form, as prohibitions against profaning the Sabbath and dishonoring parents.

The negative form of the commandments brings to our attention the frequent complaint about the negative tone of the law and of all religion that takes it seriously. It is objected that wherever the Decalogue has made its impression, a gloominess of spirit has been breathed into religion. What are we to make of this criticism? It is possible to argue that where this has happened it has arisen from a mistake of understanding, from a failure to perceive the relationship between structure and freedom. We have spoken above of the positive relationship between grace and freedom. That same positivity exists between law and freedom. The commandments do not restrict freedom but create it. People who feel that a free humanity is incompatible with a structure of law confuse human freedom with freedom from community. By so doing they end up espousing the kind of empty, abstract freedom of which we spoke earlier. To be free from community is to be utterly alone.

Those who see only the negative form of the law and therefore understand it as bondage are looking at it minus the living relationships to God and to neighbor out of which it arises. Rather, the law functions to keep community intact and whole so that men and women and children can live confidently and creatively. This is the positive behind the negative: In negativity is freedom! Thus the prohibitions can be seen to be "freers of space." The child who at one stage vexes against the parental "no" is apt, with maturity, to understand the manifold richness of possibility opened up by the security of that "no."

Contemporary process theology has given us insight into the relationship between divine law and freedom. We have commented above on how real freedom is always within limits and that the limits create the freedom. Without them, chaos! As a parent I exercise control over my child for the sake of freedom. When my youngest son was small, his grandmother gave him five dollars. With the money burning a hole in his tiny pocket, we went to the shopping mall. When he asked me, "What should I buy?" I said a fatherly thing: "Son, it's your money; you need to learn about choosing. Let's look around and then you can make up your mind." If in his shopping he was drawn to a red toy truck or a football, I would let him choose. Even some unwise choices I might tolerate. Five dollars worth of candy might produce stomach distress for him and a night of wakefulness for me, but for the sake of learning I might be compliant. But if he should clamor for the bright red amphetamine capsules in the druggist's case, I would say no. Such a choice would threaten the freedom he would be learning to exercise. Similarly, at home he would have the freedom to play in the house or the backyard but not in traffic, for this might mean the end of freedom.

So Nietzsche was wrong! God does not mean enslavement. God means freedom! Atheism, on the other hand, means slavery—to the overwhelming necessity to be our own gods. By the same logic, the law means freedom, and lawlessness and utter permissiveness mean paralysis. We will say more of this presently.

(3) *Their generality.* The general character of the commandments is akin to their negative nature. They are, it has been claimed, so broad as to lose much of their usefulness. Taken at face value, they provide surprisingly little guidance as to the courses of action we should take. Even the commandments that seem to be the most direct, specific, and doctrinaire—for instance, the prohibition against killing—do not specify wherein this rule applies and what forms of life—or death—it embraces. However, it is precisely their generality that makes them available to instruct us in concrete moments of decision. Life situations never repeat themselves, and the more precise and explicit a rule of conduct is, the less likely it is to fit the new moments and decisions that confront us. This is why traffic and road regulations that made good sense in horse-and-buggy days can strike us as ridiculous in the day of the automobile and the jet liner.

Specific rules quickly become dated, while general principles that arise out of the human situation and its lasting needs have a dateless character. The admonition not to put burrs under our neighbor's saddle blankets, because it is explicit, is time bound. It is irrelevant to those of us who never sit on a saddle. But "Thou shalt consider the safety and well-being of thy neighbor," because it is general, is timeless.

So once again our freedom to act responsibly toward each other and toward God is facilitated, not suppressed, by the general nature of the commandments and their consequent timelessness and universality. The way in which a legislation specific to a people, a time, or a culture loses its meaning in a different time and place is well illustrated by the Hebrew Levitical code. Many of the specific rules and regulations set forth in Israel's dietary regulations, her sanitary directions, and her legislation regulating the ownership and treatment of slaves have little usefulness today. Jesus himself did not hesitate to modify or set aside such laws. More properly—and this is significant—he *reinterpreted* them by discovering the general truth of which they were an application. For example, behind the rule against harvesting grain on the Sabbath, Jesus discerned the concern for people that underlies the final six commandments. Accordingly, he concluded that "the Sabbath was made for man and not man for the Sabbath."

What we have said also helps to account for their brevity. Indeed, Lester Meyer suggests that "the brevity is a function of their general applicability."[6] Thus both the brevity and the generality of the commandments enable them "to rise above many of the particulars of the time and space."[7] Harrelson's summary statement of the ten emphasizes their brevity and generality:

(1) There shall not be to thee other gods before me.
(2) Thou shalt not make for thyself a graven image.
(3) Thou shalt not lift up the name of the Lord thy God for mischief.
(4) Remember the sabbath day to sanctify it.
(5) Honor thy father and thy mother.
(6) Thou shalt not kill.
(7) Thou shalt not commit adultery.
(8) Thou shalt not steal.
(9) Thou shalt not answer thy neighbor as a false witness.
(10) Thou shalt not covet the household of thy neighbor.[8]

(4) *Their "di-unity."* The most striking feature of the commandments concerns what we will call their "di-unity." Even the most casual examination will identify what the old Calvinists called the "two tables" of the law. The "laws of the first table"—in our numbering, commandments one through four—are concerned with the relationship of humankind to God, while the "laws of the second table" are concerned with the relationships of human beings to other human beings. Accordingly, the first four have sometimes been called the "vertical commandments" and the final six the "horizontal commandments."

Thus the commandments as a whole set forth the two fundamental dimensions of a healthy existence within covenant, the relation to God and to the neighbor. But to call these two aspects of the Decalogue "dimensions" is to be reminded of their interdependence and inseparability and therefore of the oneness of the law. If Lehmann is right that the commandments are not prescriptive but descriptive, then the unity of the two dimensions is understandable. They do nothing less than describe the character of God and of the community he has created.

This twoness-yet-oneness has been reflected, perhaps unconsciously, by generations of artists. Virtually every artistic representation of Moses that I can recall pictures the tables of the law as a single rectangular slab of stone, but it is clearly subdivided by a scalloped or "bimodal" top margin.

This representation, of course, is of doubtful historicity—especially when the Hebrew commandments are prefaced by *Roman* numerals—but its point is clear: while there are two tablets and two dimensions, there is but one law because there is one God and one people of God. So the law as it relates us to God can never really be separated from the law as it relates us to one another. Where the vertical is intact, the horizontal will thrive.

This theme of God and neighbor is reflected throughout the Old Testament. The rupture of the relation of Adam and Eve with God precipitated the rupture of the family and of the human race. Spouse blamed spouse, nature, and God; brother rose up against brother, lineage against lineage, and the whole tawdry history of blood ensued.

The prophets saw the calamity of the kingdom of Israel as a repetition of the tragedy of the first couple in the garden. And the passion for human justice in the eight-century prophets rests on the burning conviction that the loss of the human in Israel's society means the loss of God. The summary of all goodness embraced love of God and neighbor. This is how Micah in the eighth century summarized the true religion. All that God required of Israel was to do justly and love kindness (thus the horizontal!) and to walk humbly with their God (thus the vertical!) (Mic 6:8). Amos, Micah's likely contemporary in the northern kingdom, could also reduce the requirement of God to the purity of the two dimensions: "Let justice (toward neighbor) roll down like waters and righteousness (toward God) like an ever-flowing stream" (Amos 5:24).

The prophets believed Israel's failure of community was a failure of trust in God. But it was their conviction of the persistence of God's grace that fueled their glowing visions of hope beyond failure. That is why the pages of Hosea, Isaiah, Jeremiah, Ezekiel, and Deutero-Isaiah are graced by a series of glowing visions of restored community through the steadfast mercy of their God.

But the most eloquent summation of the di-unity of the law and of the life it creates comes from the lips of Jesus. When asked about the "greatest commandment," Jesus answered by quoting the Hebrew's own summary, the great confession known as the *Shema*. These were the words spoken by every son of the law and by every Hebrew lad each morning on awaking: "You shall love the Lord with all your heart, soul, and strength." Then Jesus added, "the second is like to it: you shall love your neighbor as yourself." Far from selecting one of the ten and giving it priority over the rest, Jesus summarized the two tables of the law: love of God and love of neighbor.

(5) *The inclusiveness of the law.* If the law addresses and unites the two fundamental relations in life—the relation to God and to the world about us—then it is clear that it is inclusive. By this we mean it encompasses life in all of its aspects. If we reduce the Decalogue to a limited series of legal regulations, then it may well be seen as time bound, fragmentary, and irrelevant to the complex and novel situations of modern life. It then becomes, whatever its inherent wisdom, a more-or-less arbitrary bundle of moral insights.

This is a popular view: the commandments represent a random sampling of moral and ceremonial regulations that could have taken different form and had different contents. Some of my readers will recall a scene from a motion picture conceived by comedian Mel Brooks. In *The History of the World, Part 1*, Moses is seen descending from the mountain burdened by three stone tablets. He announces to the people, "I bring you these fifteen commandments!"

Then, "Oops!" he cries, as one tablet tumbles to the ground and shatters. Moses corrects himself: "I bring you these ten commandments!" If they constitute no fundamental wholeness, if they are random rules or moral insights, why not fifteen or five?

If it is true, as we have argued, that the ten propositions of the Decalogue are rooted in the character of God and in the community he has brought into being, then how can we escape their inclusive intention? While we can imagine a different formulation of every law, one thing is clear: no conceivable human situation can arise that the commandments do not address. On the other hand, not one of the commandments is arbitrary so that it could be dispensed with without loss. The commandments embrace life in all its dimensions.

COMMANDMENTS? WORDS? RULES? WHAT SHALL WE CALL THEM?

All we have said establishes the fact that the commandments rise above the level of mere rules for conduct. They are applicable to every conceivable human situation. What terminology best preserves this special status?

Caleb Carmichael reminds us that the common Hebrew designation, and one that is used in the Exodus 34 restatement of the Decalogue, is "word" or "saying."[9] A saying need not be a commandment, and the term could in fact be used to refer to the announcement or prologue in Exodus 20:1: "I am Yahweh your God who brought you out of the land of Egypt, out of the house of bondage." Harrelson suggests that the commandments be referred to as "norms," a suggestion with much to recommend it, for it reminds us that the purpose of the law is to shape, protect, and energize the community—in other words, to give it guidelines for loving God and neighbor. The laws then become descriptive of the true fellowship of trust and love.

We will speak of the commandments as "principles" to stress that they rise above the particularity of rules. This will free us to search for the religious and human meaning in those "laws" that might in some cases seem impossible to follow or enforce or might appear even to be meaningless today—for example, the commandment concerning Sabbath observance. We will ask how each of the commandments provides us with overarching truths of God and community that are valid for every moment of decision and every foreseeable future.

If we keep this point of anchor—that the principles set forth in the Decalogue are the principles of life with God and with one another—we will avoid the danger to which the word "principle" tempts us. We will not easily come to reverence the abstract principle above the individuals it embraces. It has happened all too frequently in human history that the lives and hopes of people have been sacrificed to "principle."

PARTICULARISM AND UNIVERSALITY: THE APPLICATION OF THE DECALOGUE

We need now to consider in greater depth a question raised at the end of the introduction and again in chapter 3. We have said that law has no meaning outside of covenant. If this is true, what bearing does it have on those who are not within the covenant? When we have discovered what the commandments meant to Israel, will we be able to find in them meaning for our lives today, and especially for the lives of those who have never consciously participated in the biblical traditions or claimed Israel's heritage? Does the law have any claim to universal significance or applicability? Or is it arrogance to suggest that a primitive, Semitic people could possess truths for a world far removed from the exodus, a world populated by people who have never known of it? Is it a meaningful thing to try applying the Ten Commandments to the modern world and to other cultures? Or, to put the question bluntly, how does the Hebrew Decalogue relate to a multicultural world?

Every claim to universal truth, however modestly set forth today, is greeted with the charge of *triumphalism*. A wholesome respect for the opinions of others, along with a sense of our own limitations of perspective, has led to an attractive modesty among biblical interpreters and theologians. One of the results of this modesty and sense of limitation in Christian theology has been a turn to confessionalism. The confessional theologian sometimes acknowledges that he speaks out of his own experience and that of his community. He makes no claims to speak for others. He is often hesitant to enter into arguments about truth claims concerned only to be heard. Nor is the confessional theologian particularly interested in "apologetic" theology, that is, theology that attempts to argue the truth of its claims or to prove them. He believes that the only true persuasion is witness.

While much of the theology of the twentieth century has had a strong confessional element, preeminently expressed by Karl Barth, perhaps the purest form of confessionalism is in the "narrative" theology of the last few decades. The present study is in some ways indebted to the notion of narrative theology. We have committed ourselves to understanding the covenant and the law from within the shared history of synagogue and church. We have spoken repeatedly of the "story," which was in fact Israel's confession of her faith.

I have already commented on the attractiveness that the notion of story has in many fields of study today, and especially in the humanities. Narrative has the power to draw people into the world it creates, and this is especially the case in a rootless society. To hear and respond, to be able to recognize and claim a story as one's own, is to experience inclusion and fellowship. One may thereby find a home for values, and this is good.

But while the appeal to "our story" is always attractive, it has sometimes been seen as a cowardly retreat from truth and reality and as a surrender of all reliable norms for life and decision. Our basic values are inscribed in our stories, are they not? We asked earlier whether our story must necessarily imply a larger, more inclusive story. Do the stories we tell provide the warmth of community and of familiarity and no more? Or do they do more than provide comfort? Do they make claims? If we are unwilling to make claims for the values we set forth in our storytelling and for the validity of their insights, do we reveal lack of earnestness?

I am convinced that every story told in earnest wants to be taken seriously as pointing to reality and truth. And I am suspicious of the kind of "metaphysical modesty"—that is, the claim to be uninterested in the larger questions of the truth—that permeates much of the literary and academic culture of which I am a part. I suspect that, behind our modesty about what the old philosophers called the "really real," the hope survives that we are doing more than "spinning yarns."

The question remains, "Is it possible to tell a story with real seriousness without implying 'truth value'?" Can we—must we—assert the validity—the *truthfulness*—of our story if it is not to lose life power? In a time when efforts to speak of ultimate reality or truth are often met with indulgent laughter or scorn, is it necessary to speak of God and truth before we can speak of love, justice, and peace? Surely Paul Sponheim is right that "faith commits suicide if it assesses itself as no more than a "useful fiction."[10]

Another way of asking this question is to wonder if the horizontal can survive and prosper without the vertical. The meaning of the current and much abused term "multicultural" is that, in the West, the religious and cultural hegemony of the Judeo-Christian tradition has largely disappeared and no single culture, ethic, or value system has arisen to take its place. Above all, no "god" has arisen in place of the God of Moses to provide a common basis for humanity or common norms by which we can govern our behavior. Can a secular society—that is, a society with horizontality but no verticality—have the resources to prevent its disintegrating into a pandemonium of isolated stories? Would the result be a world of people running around frantically shouting "I, I, I" but lacking the power to speak the "We!" of community? Would such a state of isolated individuals be, as the existentialist Jean-Paul Sartre has insisted, the very essence of hell?

It is not certain that the loss of a common story would mean the disintegration of values. Religionists have often been quick to insist that human values can't survive the "death of god." But significant human cooperation has sometimes proved possible among very different peoples, including those with many gods and those with no gods at all. Such cooperation has sometimes been on a level higher that mere mutual self-interest. A significant measure of human community may be possible on the basis of shared humanity and common sympathy. Perhaps particularism is not the death of a common future.

On the other hand, Western culture and most other world cultures have been shaped by religious or philosophical traditions that assumed a transcendent and universal basis for values. In these traditions and in the truth claims they gave rise to, notions of shared humanity largely rested. For instance, the American Declaration of Independence describes the equality of all humankind and the value of every human as "self-evident." That is, human worth doesn't have to be argued. This formative document assumes that all people can see the truth of it. It doesn't depend on any particular tradition, belief, or faith. It is ours merely because we are *human!*

But are the notions of freedom and equality quite so tradition independent? The difficulty that American liberal democracy has had in making headway outside of Western culture, with its Judaic roots, warns us to stop and think. Could it be that the equal worth of all people is scarcely self-evident apart form the origins of that idea in biblical tradition? According to that tradition, as we will see when we address the fifth commandment, the value of people arises not from something inherent in humankind, but from God's "valuing" of us.

It may be that there is a sufficient sense of common humanity to sustain society without any notion of a transcendent valuer, but it is also possible that such social and racial coherence as we seem to possess is the capital of a religious past. If so, is it subject to depletion? Elton Trueblood long ago spoke of Western society as a "cut flower civilization," a metaphor that might be instructive for our time. Much of the apparent vigor and creativity of the West, he suggested, flowed from the stored-up energy of its Judeo-Christian past. This included its ability to criticize its own narrowness and cultural arrogance in the name of a God who is the creator and valuer of all.

Did Israel's story of covenant with Yahweh have in it the power to transcend particularity and to achieve the vision of the inclusive community we earlier described? Israel herself did not seem to know, for the struggle between her sense of nation and her world sense was a long one, and it was perhaps never completely decisive. The tension between particularism and universalism was built into the very sense of calling that made her a people. The call was clear that she was to be a peculiar people. Amos asked on God's behalf, "Did I not bring Israel up from the land of Egypt?" (9:7).

The exodus, so Israel believed, had been a calling to uniqueness, to a special belonging. "God is our God," they were convinced, "and not the God of Egypt!" The covenant stresses *belonging.* "We are his people," they believed, "and *this is our law.*" It was Israel that he had drawn into his own workings, not the Philistines or the Edomites or the Syrians. Were their neighbors not lacking God's identifying mark or inclusion? Were they not *uncircumcised* Philistines?

The struggle of the Hebrews to establish themselves as a nation underlined their sense of separation from the gods of Palestine and the people who served them. It is no surprise that they came to confuse the God of the covenant with the kingdom of David and Solomon. The narrow religious nationalism that resulted was a consequence. A kind of national idolatry arose from the pomp and splendor of Solomon's kingdom, so that nation and covenant could no longer be distinguished. Thus the success of God's covenant could not be separated from the success of the nation, and they came to see God as the guarantor of Israel's triumph and her happiness. The national idolatry of the high monarchy seemed to be religious particularism triumphant.

Even after the chastening experience of captivity in Babylon, the postexilic nation could not escape this self-centered particularism and its resultant xenophobia (fear and hatred of outsiders). But there were other currents at work, because their story had implications for other stories and for the larger human story. The very character of God—of whom the covenant and the law were the paradigmatic expression—provided the dynamic.

The God of the covenant was a God who made promises and *kept* them. God could be trusted! But that meant he must be able to embrace not only Israel's history but all history. His faithfulness to the covenant depended not only on his mercy, but on his sovereign control over the whole of creation.

CREATIVITY AND UNIVERSALITY

Thus, because the exodus faith had implications for a larger story, Israel wrote her history backward! The people found their thoughts turning from their national beginnings at Sinai to the beginnings of the whole world. Accordingly, the other fundamental theme of the Hebrew story found its expression. We earlier quoted Sarna's judgment that biblical religion revolves around the two themes of creation and exodus. "The former," Sarna writes, "asserts God's undivided sovereignty over nature, the latter his hegemony over history."[11] But his sovereignty over history, and therefore his power to fulfill his promises, depended on his sovereignty over nature. It is interesting that the justification in the fourth commandment for sanctifying the Sabbath is God's role in creating the world.

Sovereignty is possible only in a world unified by the one power that stands alone. Israel's monotheism carried its own impulse to universalism. Thus it is not surprising that her tendency to particularism was challenged from the beginning by a powerful urge to embrace not only the Hebrew but also the stranger within Israel's gates. If God is both the God of creation and the God of the covenant, then what he has done at the exodus is a clue to his intention for all humankind and for nature as well. The Decalogue, as the heart of the covenant, becomes, in Lehmann's words, "paradigmatic of what God is doing in the world."[12] Ergo, he intends an *inclusive* community.

The urge to break the bounds of particularism and expand the covenant so as to embrace every neighbor and every nation keeps finding expression through Israel's history. The patriarchal stories clearly see Israel's election as filled with redemptive potential, and this is explicitly set forth in the terse rehearsal of the call to Abraham. The promise of land and nation and blessing reach their climax in the promise that in Abraham's seed "all the families of the earth shall be blessed" (Gen 12:1-4).

The disappointment of the monarchy undoubtedly fired the prophetic protest against circumscribing God and his law. Israel's first writing prophet, Amos, announced in no uncertain terms that the divine law embraced not merely Israel but Syria, Ammon, and Philistia also. His withering irony toward Israel expressed that universalism in negative language ("God cares no more about you, Israel, than he does about them!"), but it did so on the positive basis of God's action in a wider history—the history of humankind. When Amos asked the people of Samaria and Bethel his rhetorical question, "Did I not bring you up out of the land of Israel?" surely their reply was an affirmative one. But then, to their surprise, Amos asked pointedly and not without sarcasm, "And did he not lead the Philistines up from Caphtor and the Syrians from Kir?" If God was active in grace and covenant toward Israel, why would that action have ignored or excluded the other peoples of his creation? Amos suggested that in the calling and deliverance of Israel, we can discern God's intentions for all humankind.

It is only a step from Amos's cautious universalism to Jeremiah's joyous declaration of a New Covenant of forgiveness. One step more brings us to Deutero-Isaiah's ecstatic announcement of a New Exodus that would include all nations: "Turn to me and be saved, all the ends of the earth! For I am God and there is no other" (Isa 45:22).

Finally, we must return again to the questions we raised at the beginning of this section concerning whether a common humanity can endure without a basis for value in a common truth. If what Lehmann calls "a human future" requires a story that in its value-creating essentials is common to us all, then either one story must establish itself and declare its norms to be universal (and can this happen except by totalitarian imperialism), or we must find in the various stories a common affirmation that can give us a single humanity. The secret assumption of this study is that the story of a creator-covenant God still has in it the power of universality and that the Decalogue, as its "enfleshment," can provide the basis for a common humanity.

This is what Richard Niebuhr meant when he said a true revelation universalizes the law. While it may be arrogance to deny that any other story is worth telling and while it may be unseemly to suggest that only our story can be true, still to tell it is to recommend it, to suggest its universality and its permanent value. Niebuhr comments that while Christian confessionalism "must restrain its desire to prove the superiority of Christianity to other religions," it is nevertheless true that "revelation means God." The telling implies the story's importance and its truth.[13]

NOTES

[1] See for example Norman Gottwald, *The Tribes of Yahweh: A Sociology of the Religious Liberation of Israel* (Marynoll NY: Orbis Books, 1979). See also Marvin L. Chaney, "Ancient Palestinian Peasant Movements in the Formation of Premonachic Israel" in David Noel Freeman and David Frank, *Palestine in Transition* (Sheffield England: Almond Press, 1983).

[2] Walter Harrelson, *The Ten Commandments and Human Rights* (Philadelphia: Fortress Press, 1980), 42.

[3] Nahum Sarna, *Exploring Exodus: The Heritage of Biblical Faith* (Napierville IL: Alec R. Allenson, Inc., 1965), 104f.

[4] Ibid.

[5] Ibid.

[6] Lester Meyer, *The Message of Exodus* (Minneapolis: Augsburg Publishing House, 1983), 121.

[7] Ibid., 122.

[8] Harrelson, *The Ten Commandments and Human Rights*, 41.

[9] Caleb Carmichael, *The Origins of Biblical Law: The Decalogue and the Book of Covenant* (Ithaca: Cornell University Press, 1992), 25.

[10] Paul Sponheim, *Faith and Process* (Minneapolis: Augsburg Press, 1979), 24.

[11] Sarna, *Exploring Exodus*, 1.

[12] Paul Lehmann, *The Decalogue and a Human Future* (Grand Rapids: Wm. B. Eerdmans Publishing Company, 1995), 31.

[13] H. Richard Niebuhr, *The Meaning of Revelation* (New York: Collier Books, Macmillan Publishing Company, 1960), 129, 111.

Part Two

~

The Vertical
Commandments

Chapter Six

∽

But First . . .
A Word from God

Then God spoke all these words: "I am the LORD your God, who brought you out of Egypt, out of the house of slavery." (Exodus 20:1-2)

W e come at last to an examination of the contents of the Ten Commandments or Decalogue. All that was discussed in the first part of this book underlines the importance of understanding the law within its covenant setting if we are to grasp its meaning for the ancient Hebrew and—and this is perhaps our primary purpose—if we are to discern its possible meaning and value for us today.

We have discovered in the first part of this book that the context for understanding the law is by no means a simple one. Its narrative setting is Israel's story and her remembrance of her story. That story reveals that the primary content of her memory is the covenant with its twofold dimension: its binding of the people to God and to one another. But we have also seen that, insofar as the God revealed was the God of creation, the horizons of their narrative continued to enlarge and become more inclusive and universal.

I have a vivid memory of a Sunday morning when I was thirteen. Mr. Flewhardy, our Sunday school teacher, ceremoniously hung in our classroom a gold-framed, parchment copy of the Ten Commandments. He offered a Barlow pocketknife to the first member of the class who could quote them by heart. I treasured that knife for many years. I remember clearly how my recitation began: "Thou shalt have no other gods before me." Only years later did I become aware that there was a preface to these famous words.

Everything we have said in the preceding section about covenant and law, community and commandment, legalism and grace is in fact contained in the brief preface to the Decalogue quoted in italics above. The importance of this concise announcement has led some to refer to it as the first of the commandments. While it is not strictly speaking a commandment but rather a statement, it is so critical for giving meaning to the commandments following it that we must not pass over it lightly. Yet it has routinely been neglected or omitted from most statements of the Decalogue when they are printed independently of the biblical text. It is also frequently overlooked in homily and catechism. Such omission may result in part from the parallel wording of the commandments, each of which begins with the same imperative. The preface is not presented in the imperative ("Thou shalt" or "Thou shalt not") but in a simple indicative statement ("I am"). However, we will see that every imperative requires and receives its energy from the indicative. Every "Thou shalt!"—whether that of a parent to a child, a government to a citizen, or a God to his people—presupposes an "I am!" and a "Thou art!"

In part, the neglect of the preface may arise from the predisposition to think of the Decalogue as a code of rules and ordinances to govern behavior rather than a description of a living relationship between God and his covenant partners. As we have seen and as we shall continue to see, the latter is the case with regards to the Decalogue.

The book of Exodus calls the various provisions of the Decalogue "words." Caleb Carmichael suggests that the phrase "Ten Commandments" is a misnomer and that it misses the point of this Hebrew designation of "word." He writes:

> To be sure most of the ten "words" consist of commandments, but such an assessment excludes the significance that lies in the Hebrew designation. A saying may consist of more than one commandment or it may be a commandment with explanatory statements or it may consist of a statement only as in Exodus 20:2: "I am Yahweh thy God who brought thee out of the land of Egypt, out of the house of bondage."[1]

It is not surprising, therefore, that the preface is sometimes considered an integral part of the Decalogue and, indeed, the first "word" of the ten. But its simple, declarative syntax belies its energy and its multiple levels of meaning.

Thus, as we have said, to ignore this "word" is to invite distortion of the commandments themselves. Let us consider several of the aspects of this pregnant "word."

(1) *The preface as "epiphaneous."* This rather flamboyant term may awaken us again to the character of the Decalogue and of the book of Exodus as a whole. It derives from the Greek *epiphainein,* meaning to "show forth." Most Christians will recognize the word as it is used in reference to the season of Epiphany in the Christian year. Accordingly, an epiphany is a "showing forth," a divine moment of confrontation in which life is forever altered by the luminous presence of God. Paul Tillich has rendered the same notion with a powerful German word that almost translates itself; he speaks of the *Hereinbrechen* (The "breaking-into-here") of God.

To speak of Exodus as an epiphaneous book, then, means to be aware of its veritable saturation with the divine glory. Johnstone reminds us that the book of Exodus is a confession. Far from being a neutral and objective setting forth of events, it is the Hebrews' awestruck account of having been "seized upon" by God.[2]

The epiphany of God throws light on the commandments that follow. Consider the role played in Exodus by the image of light. In fact, throughout the Old Testament as a whole, few symbols of God are more omnipresent than that of light or its corollary, fire. God's first creative act is described in Genesis 1:3 as the bringing of light into darkness, and the divine barrier to the fallen couple at the gate of paradise is depicted as a flashing or flaming sword. Similarly, the two cognate symbols blend in Isaiah's solemn warning to the people that "the Light of Israel will become a fire and his Holy One a flame" (Isa 10:17). The imagery is also found prominently in the New Testament and particularly in the Nativity narratives (the star in Matthew and the divine glory upon the shepherds in Luke,) in the narrative of the transfiguration in the three synoptic Gospels, and in the account of the divine epiphany on the day of Pentecost (Acts 2:1-4).

The message is clear: Where there is light, there is God! No book in the Hebrew Bible is more radiant with the sense of light as the divine presence than Exodus. A "halo" surrounds Israel's memory and her recounting of those days that saw the birth of freedom, nation, and Decalogue. The initial event from which this sense of divine presence seems to radiate is the burning (glowing?) bush. Yahweh continues throughout the book to shed his light on Israel. The "glowing cloud"—the *kabod* glory of God—that leads them in their wilderness journey is the divine presence upon and among them. It is the same "glory of the Lord" that fills the tabernacle upon its dedication (Exod 40:34-37). And the actual receiving of the Decalogue finds the Lord descending upon the mountain in smoke and fire (19:18).

Thus as the Hebrew story was remembered and internalized, both covenant and law were born in the white heat of the divine presence. This must not be forgotten. Indeed, whether in the final analysis the commandments can have meaning for our day may depend in no small measure on whether the quality of the transcendent, the "epiphaneous," is any longer available to us. There may be no power in law for that society in which there is "no frequent vision."

(2) *The preface as divine self-description.* Perhaps we can enlarge on Lehmann's distinction between the law as prescriptive and descriptive. We could speak of the indicative (what *is*) and of the imperative (what we are to *do*). But the imperative depends on the indicative. The character of God is the clue to what life should be. This distinction explains why some commentators like Lehmann are uncomfortable with the use of the word "code" to describe the Decalogue. To call it a "code of laws" suggests a rulebook understanding. But he has proposed another more fruitful way of understanding the commandments as a code. He writes:

> We are drawn not under the rules but into parables. The word *code* denotes not a repository of regulations but the clue to responsibilities. The Decalogue underlines the *indicative,* in distinction from the legalistic, the *descriptive* as opposed to the prescriptive relation of the Commandments to the human living of human life. The tone of the Decalogue is not: "This is what you had better do or else!" On the contrary, the tone is rather: "Seeing that you are who you are, where you are, and as you are, this is the way ahead, the way of being and living in truth, the way of freedom."[3]

Codes are clues to responsibilities! Again, we must not forget that responsibilities are *response-abilities*—they point to our ability to respond—and are dependent for their existence on the realities to which we are called to respond. The burden of Lehmann's treatment is the quality of human existence. The book itself is subtitled "The Meaning of the Commandments for Making and Keeping Life Human." In other words, they are descriptive of the quality of the humanity toward which they point.

But it is surely the case that only God can define the quality of life. His very being determines value at the human level. God's character is contained in the words, "I am the LORD your God *that brought you out of the land of Egypt.*" In other words, the law is not only *descriptive* (of the way human existence ought to be) but *self-descriptive* (of the way God is). To know God in the fullest possible way is to know the law in living presence, not as dictates but as reality. To have the law, even in Israel's imperfect and benighted way, was to have the surest clue to knowing God.

But this conclusion opens up to Lehmann a new and helpful way of thinking of the commandments as a code. He draws his insight from Robert Penn Warren's haunting observation that "the whole world pours at us, but the codebook, somehow is lost."[4] Lehmann suggests that the Decalogue is indeed a code insofar as it opens up and makes readable the impenetrable mystery and chaos of human life in all ages, but especially modern life. There is a universal pathos in Warren's lament for all who have stood baffled, unable to decipher the situations that confront them. We have all longed for codebook, a key that would unlock life's mystery.

In a recent seminar session with a group of undergraduates, I proposed a question of how, in the current multicultural and multivalue environment, a person could make artistic or moral value judgments. In other words, is it possible any longer to suggest that one piece of art, one song or musical composition, one standard of worth could be given any priority over another? Many of the students were unwilling to express an opinion. Others were unwilling to say that Shakespeare's *Hamlet* was superior to a skit on *Saturday Night Live* or that Mozart's *The Marriage of Figaro* (portions of which they had just heard) was artistically more worthy than a performance by Madonna. Not superior, they added, only different. When pressed on moral or ethical issues, rather than aesthetic, they seemed even less able to unravel the mysteries. One young man, impatient with the whole discussion, concluded, "Don't ask me to comment of the rightness or wrongness of anything. I haven't got a clue!"

It may be that there has never been an age that has stood more clueless in the face of the future. How does one begin to move toward human and societal wholeness in such a world? If the Decalogue is a clue to the character of God, then it is a clue to the meaning of human life under God and with one another. Lehmann suggests that it is indeed the lost codebook that can unlock the mystery of a human future.

(3) *The preface as claim.* Moses at the bush stood on "holy ground." So did the people at Sinai. The word of the preface is not mere declaration. It is not merely indicative or even descriptive. The preface, for all its simple indicative

form, has imperative force. *It is demand.* It presents itself as fact and leaves to one side all consideration of options. *It is irresistible.*

The Hebrew affirmation of God's act of election is the root of one of the most widely debated issues in the history of biblical religion—one that we addressed above: that of the irresistibility of grace. Is grace irresistible? If we are to take God's initiative and faithfulness seriously, then in some essential way it must be so! Can God move in the world and the world not be moved? There can surely be no question about our responding to his grace, but what does the notion of grace imply? The confusion may clear somewhat when we remember that the demand is essentially a demand *to respond*! Our response embraces all the options and possibilities that freedom makes available. That these options are not endless goes without saying. Indeed, it has been said in previous chapters. But God's calling focuses those possibilities and makes them concrete and real.

How we respond to election is, within the limits, ours to determine; *whether* we respond is not. We can no more be embraced by election and grace and not respond than we can be on the earth and not rest our feet on its surface. So, as we have already seen, the demand is at the same time the beginning of freedom. I may respond in many ways, but I cannot remain untouched by his elective embrace.

(4) *The preface as affirmation.* "What's in a name? That which we call a rose, by any other name, would smell as sweet." Romeo's attempt to escape from the name of Montague is as adolescent as it is futile. The Hebrew respect for names and the sense of outrage when a name was taken "in vain" arose in part from the conviction that in some sense a name is inseparable from the person named. For the Hebrew, a person's name encapsulates the character of the person who bears it. To make light of another's name or to use it disrespectfully was to insult or demean the person. Also, because of the intimate connection between one's name and one's identity, character, and worth, a change of name—as in the cases of Abram and Jacob—was fraught with meaning. In both cases, the changing of the name was the climactic event of a whole life. If the name enshrined the person's character and status, then the intoning of a new name was the declaration of a new person.

Thus the pronouncing of one's own name could be either blessing or cursing; it could be community-creating and value-bestowing, or it could be threat. It could communicate beneficence or malignancy, depending on the character of the one whose name was invoked.

In interpersonal life, the giving of one's name is an act of self-bestowal. Indeed, the initial act in all human relations involves the giving of the name: "Hello, I'm Anne." Such giving is at once an invitation to community and a sacrifice of the splendid isolation of self. As such, it is an act of self-risk, since to be known is to be vulnerable. The person who knows my name possesses some degree of power over me. This is why most cultures have their legends of name discovery.

Richard Wagner's opera *Lohengrin* is built around such a legend. Lohengrin, a knight of the Holy Grail, is sent from Montsalvat as champion of the falsely accused Elsa of Brabant. On promise that Elsa never ask him his name, he takes her as his bride. However, the mystery proves too much for the innocent but human Elsa, who, tormented by her doubts, at last asks of him his name. Lohengrin denounces her failure and sadly returns to Montsalvat.

Wagner intends a contrast between the high, holy—even self-sacrificing— character of the knight and the weakness of the "eternal feminine." But the listener is not apt to direct his admiration and sympathy toward Lohengrin. Is Elsa to be faulted for asking, even against her promise, to know her husband's name? When he withholds his name from her he withholds himself. He deprives her of full identity and denies true community to their marriage. Despite the employment of Christian and biblical themes in this opera, Wagner reveals his profound ignorance of the meaning of those themes. There is nothing particularly sacred or sublime in self-isolation, and this is as true of God as it is of Lohengrin.

There is nothing inherently sacred in the "divine incognito." The one who is truly God is not God *in se* ("in himself"), remote and above all character and name, but the God *pro nobis,* ("for us"). It is the pronouncement, "I am Yahweh, your God," that affirms and embraces Israel. It is the "I am your father" that carries with it the message, "You are my children." The preface of the Decalogue does not merely demand: it also affirms and it bestows.

(5) *The preface as creative and "time-binding" power.* God's pronouncing of his name at Sinai—first to Moses at the burning bush and then later through him to the people—is the beginning of Israel's story. Nothing seems more evident from the Old Testament accounts.

Before receiving "the name," Israel was not a people and had neither covenant nor law. The giving of the name launches both. The loss of the name—if it should ever come to be—would be the end of the story. This is the point of Amos's consigning of the citizens of Samaria to the ash-heap of history. All of their burnt offerings and rivers of oil and all their pious longing for the "Day of the Lord" could not obscure the fact that they had lost the name. The God they were calling on was not the God who had met Moses at Sinai, and so the Day of the Lord for them would be darkness and not light. It would be the end of their story.

If the name of God and his manifestation of himself creates story, it also embraces and sanctifies time. God's epiphany and his action in Israel's history banished any uncertainty about whether time is real or significant for God. The notion that God does not participate in or experience time but dwells in some kind of timeless eternal present is wholly unbiblical and does no justice either to God or to history. The story of Israel was important because it was God's story too. The biblical God is a God immersed in time and thus a God with a past ("I am the God of your fathers") and a future ("I will go before you"). To have only the "eternal present" is to have no story at all.

When Yahweh gave Israel his name at the burning bush, he gave her a heritage. When I bestow my name upon my child, I bestow at the same time a heritage. As my son or my daughter, my child receives a past that predates his or her birth and gives richness and significance to the child's present being. My daughter has great-grandparents and ancestors who, though she will never know them, shape her identity and give meaning to her decisions. My son has a place (he is a Texan!) and a people (he is an American!). When he asks me, "Who am I?" and I answer, "You are my boy," I bestow upon him a past as well as a present.

I also open up to him the possibility of a definite and concrete future and thus the possibility of free choice and human morality. The capacity for transcending the present, for remembering the past, and giving creative shape to the future appears to be uniquely human. Gordon Kaufman has said that man is a "time-binder." This transcendence of the moment sets us apart from the animals and is at least in part what it means to be in the image of God.

It is also the essence of story. A story begins "once upon a time" and ends, hopefully, in happiness "ever after." But the truthfulness of a story is finally in its power to create community and to shape the future. The family heritage, when it is no longer able to stir my children or their children and to create present worth and future hope, is quickly lost to memory.

In the exodus experience, Israel inherited a history. But it should be stressed that it was not merely the history of the patriarchs that they received; it was God's own history. In the preface to the Decalogue, Yahweh identifies his name with his action. The declaration "I am Yahweh who brought you out of the land of Egypt, out of the house of bondage" is not really a reminder of his past action. It is current. What is at that moment happening to the people at the mountain is part of the bush and the Passover and the deliverance at the sea. It is all one great redemptive present, but it has implications for all cosmic pasts and all eschatological futures. It is God's story.

So it is with every act of divine self-manifestation, every epiphany. The declaration has a past and a future. Just as the burning bush is not the beginning of God or of his dealing with Israel, so Sinai is not the beginning of people and covenant. It is the present word that recalls past and opens up the future. The "once upon a time" fades into fantasy unless it is renewed in the epiphaneous present. It also is the power of the future. As we have seen, the exodus experience turned the Hebrew mind back to creation and turned it forward to new creation. At this point, story began to become history and gave rise to the deep feeling of biblical faith for the reality and meaning of time.

NOTES

[1] Caleb Carmichael, *The Origins of Biblical Law: The Decalogue and the Book of Covenant* (Ithaca: Cornell University Press, 1992), 25.

[2] W. Johnstone, *Exodus* (Sheffield England: JSOT Press, 1990), 39.

[3] Paul Lehmann, *The Decalogue and a Human Future* (Grand Rapids: Wm. B. Eerdmans Publishing Company, 1995), 41-42.

[4] Ibid.

Chapter Seven

~

The First Commandment

The Character of God

You shall have no other gods before me.
(Exodus 2:3)

et God be God! The phrase is Martin Luther's. It occurs with variations throughout his writings but especially in reference to the first commandment. Luther's passion for stating and restating this initial commandment arises from his reaction to the elaborate system of self-salvation that had arisen on the structure of late medieval Catholicism. Out of his own discovery of religion as grace he had come to see every form of legalism as a usurpation of God's role. So, as he saw it, the beginning of true wisdom was for humankind to surrender to the sovereignty and grace of God. To do otherwise was to repeat the error of the original couple in the garden. They believed it was possible to give meaning to their own existence, to be their own Gods! For Luther, the message of the first commandment is to forsake that hopeless task and to *let God be God.*

Thus the first commandment defines the relationship between man and God by defining the character of God. The definition contains a warning against both Eden and Babel. The most pervasive temptation of humankind is to assert the unity of life under the sovereignty of the self. ("Ye shall be as God!") But the ironic consequence of every such effort is the disintegration and fragmentation of life into a Babel or into isolation and fear, into a turmoil of pathetic voices, each one crying out into the silence its own name.

As seen in the biblical story, there is a linear connection between Eden and Babel, between self-worship and polytheism, a connection that we need to explore further in the pages that follow.

The first commandment, that Israel is to have no other gods before Yahweh, speaks to the human longing for wholeness and therefore for purpose in our existence. Beyond argument, this commandment is the most direct and specific root of Near-East monotheism. Out of that root, the three great monotheistic religions have sprung: Hebraism, Christianity, and Islam. Thus the principle of monotheism is more than a numerical principle; it is rather a principle for the organization of life and for escape from chaos. Monotheism is about meaning in human life.

And yet, as we have seen, it has been questioned whether the people to whom the commandment was addressed could be properly called monotheists. Indeed, Moses' own monotheism has been called in question. It has sometimes been suggested that at best he could be called a *henotheist*.

Does the biblical evidence allow us to answer the question as it relates to Moses and the exodus community? Was Moses a monotheist? Were the Hebrews of the Exodus period and the centuries immediately thereafter worshipers of and believers in one god? The language of the first commandment seems to leave the question open: "You shall have no other gods *before* me." Lester Meyer echoes a common view when he expresses the opinion that as stated it does not deny that there are other gods.[1]

Walter Harrelson is even more specific; he is of the opinion that Exodus 20:3 assumes the reality of other gods. He writes: "[The first commandment] doesn't presuppose a monotheistic position on the part of the author. Rather, it presupposes the existence of other gods."[2] He points out that the Hebrew expression *'el panay*, commonly rendered "before me," merely prohibits Israel from taking as rivals to Yahweh any of the other deities of the ancient Near-Eastern world. If he is correct, then the Mosaic position would seem to be almost a textbook case of henotheism.

Sarna, however, disagrees with this interpretation. In his view, to read the *'el panay* of Exodus 20:3 in this way is to ignore the sustained warfare waged against polytheism, not only in the Decalogue but in Exodus as a whole and in the entirety of Hebrew history. Indeed, he has no difficulty in seeing Moses as the primary, if not the only, really potent and lasting source of Middle East and

Western monotheism: If he is right, the expression "before me" takes on the force and meaning of "besides me," or "other than me." Sarna writes:

> It is the arrival of Moses on the scene of history that heralds the first appearance of a war on polytheism, expressed by the statement in Exodus 12:12: "I will mete out punishments to all the gods of Egypt, I the Lord." The Ten Commandments clearly and unambiguously mandate the absolute prohibition on polytheism and idolatry for the entire people of Israel: You shall have no other gods besides me.[3]

How do we decide who is right? What does the first commandment mean? We can probably reach a final conclusion only when we consider how this commandment affects and shapes the whole Hebrew perspective on the world. Still, we can move toward a working understanding by asking the question that seems to be at the heart of the issue: Is life unified by a power that can defy chaos and meaninglessness and make possible purpose and hope, or is it not? If the answer is "yes," then our judgment in chapter 2 is reinforced. Taken on these terms, Sarna is surely right. Whether Moses can be considered a *theoretical* monotheist is a matter of limited importance. It seems clear that he is a *practical* monotheist. From the opening pages of Exodus, it is clear that whatever beings there might be that other peoples called gods, they were totally helpless when confronted by the God of the exodus. If they existed at all, they were demoted to the status of demons—and impotent ones, at that—when faced with the power of Yahweh.

In such a practical monotheism lay the seeds of the powerful and pure theoretical monotheism that was to become such a distinctive mark of Israel's later prophets. Harrelson himself locates the impetus for that development in the exclusive demands of the first commandment. Israel is forbidden to take as a rival to Yahweh any other gods because, as concerns the power of being, *they do not matter.* To be powerless—to be unable to impress oneself on the world or on others—is tantamount to nonexistence. If a thing has no power to make itself felt or known, in what way can it be said to *be?* Yet the utter powerless of the gods of Egypt is precisely what is implied by the first commandment. Harrelson concludes that "the commandment makes clear the community of Israel is not to credit such gods with any significant power over their lives."[4]

Therefore even a practical monotheism—if that is what Moses' was—had within it the dynamic for a pure or theoretical monotheism. Yahweh's claim to exclusive worship arose out of his self-manifestation and his sovereign control over the gods of Egypt and, as expressed in the saga of the ten plagues, over the natural processes that they symbolized. Therefore the sovereignty of the exodus God quickly came to be seen as embracing the whole of creation.

Sarna sees the first commandment as utterly unique in the religious history of the Near East, both in its demand and in its revolutionary and innovative nature.[5] This seems to be a justified assertion, at least on the basis of the Hebrew story. Sarna argues that the sustained attack on idolatry that characterizes the whole of Hebrew history originated with the exodus. Despite accounts in the rabbinic literature that describe Abraham as an iconoclast, nothing in the patriarchal narratives suggests it. Moses is the great smasher of idols; the unending warfare expressed in the plague stories in Egypt and in the account of the golden calf at Sinai flows from him. The same warfare is present in the demand placed upon Israel by Joshua as Israel was settling the land: "Choose for yourselves whom you will serve, whether the gods your forefathers served beyond the river, or the gods of the Ammonites in whose land you are living" (Josh 24:15).

The response of the people makes it clear that their choice rests on practical grounds, namely, the power and faithfulness of God:

> Far be it from us that we should forsake the LORD to serve other gods; for it is the LORD our God who brought us and our ancestors up from the land of Egypt, out of the house of slavery, and who did these great signs in our sight. He protected us along the way that we went and among all the peoples through whom we passed. . . . Therefore we also will serve the LORD, for he is our God. (Josh 24:16-18)

This campaign against idolatry in all its forms was taken up by the prophets, not only against the gods of their neighbors but against the Hebrew nation itself when it began to usurp the allegiance due only to God. It reached perhaps its most powerful expression in Deutero-Isaiah's scathing indictment of those exiled Hebrews that would dare to confuse Yahweh with Bel or Marduk, the gods of the Chaldeans. (See Isa 40:18-20; 9:13-20; 45:16-22.)

Monotheism versus Monism

All of this means that the first commandment is a repudiation of every form of dualism and a denial of anything that claims to have the power to frustrate the redemptive purposes of God. Accordingly Harrelson can rephrase it in this way: "Thou shalt not deny that being is one."[6] Any form of ultimate dualism, any denial that being is one, is a dashed hope. This is the *religious* meaning of monotheism: there is nothing that can claim being or power over against God. But this does not mean that finite powers don't exist or finite beings don't matter. Biblical monotheism is not monism, in which finally every self-determining free act is a delusion! As we have seen, Hebrew monotheism affirms the reality of the world and the power of free creatures to act, to change the world, and to actually qualify God himself.

The distinction between monotheism and monism is important. In a true monism, such as is found in some of the "India born" religions, in certain expressions of first century Gnosticism, and in some forms of Christian mysticism, every finite thing is a manifestation of the one true reality. Nothing has any independent existence or power on its own. In such a view, the material world and all life within it is finally an illusion, and the human self, an emanation and a fleeting expression of the one spirit, is destined for reabsorption into the divine. Thus our existence, if it can be called existence at all, is conditional at best, and time and history are the realm of unreality.

Tillich is correct that the notion of an all-encompassing and all-consuming oneness is not the heritage of the "Israel-born religions."[7] Thus the equating of the finite world with illusion is foreign to them. It is also foreign to biblical religion to seek an answer to the problem of finitude by the absorbing of the finite into the infinite, undifferentiated *one.* In a biblical monotheism, the oneness of God is not a metaphysical oneness that excludes the reality of the creature. It is the organic oneness of the living God who holds together nature and history and gives them permanent value and meaning. The biblical symbol is not *absorption,* in which all finite differences vanish, but *reconciliation,* in which difference is preserved and enhanced in a fuller whole.

Hebrew Monotheism and the Trinity

Our comments about monism should help us to clear up a common misunderstanding about Hebrew and Christian theology. The God of the exodus is one God: this is the heart of the Hebrew confession. Then what are we to make of the Christian confession that God is "three-in-one"? How are we to understand the doctrine that to many sets a yawning, impassable chasm between the two biblical faiths? This is not the place for an extended discussion of the doctrine that, despite its importance, has mystified as many Christians as it has Jews. First, let us remember the distinction we have made on several occasions between a religious intuition and the doctrine that expresses it. We must always make an effort to catch the religious affirmation behind any doctrinal expression. It may be that the affirmations of Hebrew and Christian have much in common even though their language differs.

Second, let no man doubt that Christians stand with their Jewish fellows in regard to the first commandment. *Christians are monotheists!* The notion of God's threefold nature is not a metaphysical proposition but a confessional one. It affirms God's *dynamic, living* oneness. His is not the empty oneness of monism or the chaotic disunity of polytheism. His oneness is the organic oneness of a loving, active creator God. It is true that the notion of the Trinity cannot be found in the Hebrew Scriptures, but the doctrine of the "living God" can. Unlike a stone or an abstraction, a living being is a constantly changing unity-in-diversity, with the capacity to receive and embrace every new thing and every new experience without losing its oneness. The metaphor of the living God points to this unity-in-diversity, and the doctrine of the Trinity seeks to express it. Therefore the essential elements out of which the church was to forge its Trinitarian faith are abundantly present in the faith of Israel.

On Being Our Own Gods

The meaning, then, of the first commandment is to let God really *be* God, because the cost of refusing to do so is the fractionalizing and trivializing of life in both its vertical and horizontal dimensions. "Stop trying to be your own God!" So reads the imperative of the first commandment. It warns that the unbearable burden of being our own gods crushes out gratitude and love toward both God and the neighbor.

How does that burden alter our ability to perceive and to love God? The heroic and yet pathetic struggle to be our own God transforms God's face. We see him as the enemy of our freedom and self-determination. Nietzsche argued that humankind must kill God; otherwise, how could we bear it to be no Gods? In our puny pretensions, we see only what Luther called "the strange face of God." When we are striving to be God, God becomes the interferer, the one who comes upon us, lays siege to the citadels of ego we have built, and demands that we yield. Rather than loving him, we learn to hate him for his demand. Because we carry the burden of being our own gods, we dare not look behind that mask that we have put upon him to find his true face, the face of grace.

The story of the fall in Genesis 3 makes this point clearly and with psychological acuteness. The heart of the serpent's temptation is not merely to violate a divine regulation but to "be like God, knowing good and evil." When at last the couple yields, the countenance of God is transformed. He who had been giver of life and paradise becomes threat. Yet it is clear in the account that it is not, in fact, God who has changed but the couple's perception of him.

After the fall, God is depicted as coming to the garden to have communion with them. The picture is one of divine equanimity and beneficence, not one of retributive wrath, as he appears walking among the trees of the garden in the "cool of the day." But the communion can no longer be, not because God has turned his face away but because his creatures have turned theirs away. It is they, not God, who hide themselves among the trees of the garden. God has not even, so to speak, cleared his throat to utter words of judgment, but Adam and Eve see him already as threat and judge.

"Let God be God" as Threat and Promise

The first four commandments were succinctly summarized in the *Shema*, the great confession that every devout Jew uttered with a solemn countenance: "Hear O, Israel, the LORD is one, and thou shalt love the LORD thy God with all thy heart." As the second commandment will remind us, God is a jealous God, one who exacts from his worshipers their whole hearts. The oneness of God therefore comes as a threat to all who would divide their allegiance to him. God's creative righteousness is at the heart of the wholeness of life.

Luther's passion for the first commandment is the reason for his attack on the self-serving, man-centered legalism into which late medieval Christianity so often degenerated. He believed so strongly that the center of religion is God and not man that he offered the opinion that a true believer would sacrifice even his own soul if it would please God. That Christian is to be considered, in Luther's word, a dubious one unless he is willing to be "damned for the glory of God."

This strange and harsh-sounding judgment reminds us that in the last analysis we are not God and that neither our own happiness nor even our salvation matter in the scheme of things more than God himself. But Luther's harshness conceals grace, just as the strange face of God conceals his true face. I have sometimes observed with a touch of irony that in the end, for Luther, the only kind of God he would be willing to be damned for the glory of was a God who didn't go around damning people for his glory. In other words, only one who knows God as grace can utterly trust his destiny to him. It should be remembered that "You shall have no other Gods before me" is subsumed under "I am the Lord your God."

"Let God be God" may have the sound of overshadowing threat—and indeed it is a threat to our desire to be god. It is the divine "No!" spoken in order that that futile and ultimately self-defeating desire might be exposed for what it is. But in closing off that possibility, it opens us to grace, to letting God be God. To use the frequently uttered words of Karl Barth, it is the divine "No!" that is at the same time the divine "Yes!"

Luther's discovery of the divine Yes behind the No was the catalyst of his whole theological system. He had been taught to think of the righteousness of God as that which stood in awesome judgment on all his feeble efforts. God was being righteous, and therefore, true to his own character, when he confronted humankind as judge and exacted retribution. The turning point for Luther was his discovery that the righteousness of God expressed not only God's wrath but also his mercy. If, indeed, God's righteousness is that which sets him apart from his sinful creatures, then God is least like humankind and most like himself in his mercy. The call of God for man's total allegiance is a call to freedom and grace.

To put it in yet another way, the call to "Let God be God," encompasses the whole character of God. Thus it embraces his trustworthiness (an idol is not to be trusted) and his graciousness. It is therefore, as we seem driven to say again and again, a call to freedom. When we are able to let God be God we ourselves will be able to be human and to let others be human too.

NOTES

[1] Lester Meyer, *The Message of Exodus* (Minneapolis: Augsburg Publishing House, 1983), 122.

[2] Walter Harrelson, *The Ten Commandments and Human Rights* (Philadelphia: Fortress Press, 1980), 54.

[3] Nahum Sarna, *Exploring Exodus: The Heritage of Biblical Faith* (Napierville IL: Alec R. Allenson, Inc., 1965), 144.

[4] Harrelson, *The Ten Commandments and Human Rights.*

[5] Sarna, *Exploring Exodus*, 136-40.

[6] Harrelson, *The Ten Commandments and Human Rights*, 60.

[7] Paul Tillich, *Systematic Theology*, vol. 3 (Chicago: University of Chicago Press, 1963), 400.

Chapter Eight

~

The Second Commandment

Concerning Idols

You shall not make any graven image, or any likeness of anything that is in heaven above, or that is in the earth beneath, or that is in the water under the earth; you shall not bow down to them or serve them; for I the LORD your God am a jealous God, visiting the iniquity of the fathers upon the children to the third and the fourth generation of those who hate me, but showing steadfast love to thousands of those who love me and keep my commandments.
(Exodus 20:4-6)

The second commandment as it appears in the received text is the most extensive of the ten. However, the explanatory text is probably a later interpretation. Harrelson suggests that originally it might have read, "Thou shalt not make for thyself a graven image," or even more briefly, "Thou shalt not make for thyself an idol."[1]

In discussing this commandment separately from the first we follow the common practice in most of the Protestant community. However, in the older Catholic tradition—a tradition followed by Luther but not by Calvin—the prohibition of idolatry was treated as a part of the first commandment. The number of ten was preserved by a division into two parts of the commandment against coveting. The content is the same in either case.

While we will treat the first and second commandments separately, the argument for considering them as one is obvious. Indeed, much that was said in the previous section could as easily have found its place in this section. We can understand the second commandment as making clear the practical consequences of failure to fulfill the first.

THE "GOLDEN CALF": IMAGES OF THE HOLY

Some Old Testament scholars have seen the golden calf episode described in Exodus 32 as the specific situation to which the prohibition of idolatry was addressed. For instance, Carmichael suggests that the preface to the Decalogue is intended to contrast Yahweh with the idol Aaron presented to Israel. This is the God, Aaron told them, who has "brought you out of Egypt." The words of Moses then stand in contrast: it is not the calf, but Yahweh who has done this and therefore he claims their unswerving allegiance. Carmichael also sees the explanation for the warnings and promises contained in the second commandment as referring respectively to the loyal Levites and the rebellious people. It is clear, however, that the impact of the prohibition was not limited in subsequent Hebrew tradition to this one episode. It was generalized to govern all relations of the world, the people and God.

The second commandment has sometimes been understood as a protest against all representations, whether in religion or in life as a whole. This understanding has been a powerful influence in Islam, where portraiture and explicit representation of natural objects has often been forbidden, not merely in worship, but also in art, architecture, and decoration. This restriction has in no wise crippled the creative imagination, as anyone can affirm who has seen the powerful use of geometric abstractions in Moorish or Arabic architecture, not to mention the calligraphic beauty of the Arabic language itself. However, the notion that the monotheism of the first commandment and the prohibition against idols in the second excludes all forms of representation never seems to have been the Hebrew understanding. Representative art had a significant place in Hebrew society.

But does the second commandment prohibit all symbolic representation of God or the use of images in the context of *worship*? No, not even that! The history of Israel seems to make this clear. Representational objects found their place in the cultic life of Israel, such as the bronze bulls that figured prominently in the Solomonic temple and the cherubic and angelic figures that decorated its walls and embraced the ark of the covenant.

Nor did the Hebrew think for a moment that any speech about God could be comprehended without the concrete imagery that is the heart of all meaningful language. The Hebrews were not so foolish as to believe they could enhance the stature of the concrete God by impoverishing all language about him. If the Hebrews' use of visual representations in worship was poor by comparison with some of the other religions of the Near East, they seem to have compensated by a remarkable richness of verbal representation. The imagery of brass and stone was augmented by the imagery of words.

The reader will recall our earlier discussion of the metaphoric nature of language. There we argued that all religious language is essentially an effort to conceive of and to speak symbolically of the "unsymbolizable." But we have already learned that we must try to symbolize him who would seem to defy symbolic expression. We need merely to keep in mind this distinction: It is one thing to take seriously the warning of the second commandment against images that stand "in the place" of God; it is another thing to adopt the kind of iconoclasm that sees the objects of the world as hostile to the religious sense and as incapable of communicating God. The Hebrew held no such negative view of nature. It was God's own world. There is nothing inherently irreligious or idolatrous about religious imagery.

Harrelson reminds us that religious images are not a mark of crudity or primitivism. On the contrary, "Making representatives of the divine powers is a highly sophisticated religious practice and rests upon a well-developed understanding of how the transcendence of God is to find its depiction here on the material earth."[2] The human power to grasp the dimension of mystery in life is immeasurably pauperized by the loss of the symbolizing power of the mind. The second commandment says nothing against image and symbol except when they become devices by which we can avoid the claim of God—in other words, when images become idols.

The price we pay for confusing idolatry with symbol-making is often a literalism in religious thought that can be fatal to a sense of the holy. In worship this may take the form of a removal of all visual and tactile stimuli, such as was sometimes done in Calvinist and Quaker communities. In such cases, plainness and even barrenness were the ultimate virtues. In extreme cases, effort has been made to suppress religious poetry and any sort of rhetorical or musical "enhancement" of the plain, historical meaning of Scripture. The kind of verbal literalism often associated with the doctrine of biblical inerrancy is one consequence. We may suggest two reasons why the literalist mentality represents a misguided understanding of the biblical warning against image-making:

(1) Literalism is not really an option. It cannot be carried through. Even the most rigorous biblical literalist will fall back on and acknowledge the metaphoric nature of biblical language. I know of none who are concerned about the mineral constitution of Peter, whose name designates him as "rock." It is the case that the richest development of the rhetoric of faith in preaching has taken place in the Calvinist tradition. Meaning requires images!

(2) To the extent that such literalism is achieved, it is apt to produce a mind with a greatly reduced capacity for experiencing and comprehending God. Iconoclasm has its point, but it can degenerate into a deadly, spirit-killing thing. It can become the death of *epiphany*. The Hebrew knew the value of object and word, image and metaphor for opening up the mind and heart to reality. The acted symbolism of scapegoat and burnt offering, the richness of imagery in the Psalms—which, it should be remembered, were employed in worship—and the physical imagery of serpent, ark, ascending smoke, and holy mountain—all of these should make it clear that the prohibition of idolatry was not meant to desacralize the world, *except when that world became confused with God.* For the Hebrew the world was the ultimate sacrament; it was God's world and the arena for the working out of his purposes.

The kind of militant anti-sacramentalism sometimes encountered in Protestantism has arisen from the legitimate fear that sacramental religion can decline into idolatry. But it should not be confused with the biblical perspective. The world of the Bible is a sacramental world where bushes burn and asses speak more than they know. The second commandment is intended not to deny the epiphaneous power of the world but to prevent us from worshiping the world instead of the God who makes himself known through the world.

In this context, Paul Tillich's classic insight into the two great mainstreams of Christian faith, the Catholic and the Protestant, is helpful.[3] Each has its special genius, he tells us. The genius of Catholic Christianity, whether Orthodox or Roman, is what he calls the "Catholic substance"; that is, the sense of the holy. The Catholic is capable of discerning the presence of God in every finite fact and moment—in relic and holy water, in altar and roadside shrine, in celebration and in grief. It has been said that, as with sacred art of the Middle ages, there is a "halo" of the divine presence hovering around things Catholic. This aura of the holy is what gives its particular flavor to Catholic faith and practice.

But its genius is also the source of its greatest temptation: to confuse the sacred object or image with God. What qualifies an object as a true symbol or sacrament is its ability to make God's presence real. A true symbol is transparent; we see through it to God. However, an image easily loses its transparency.

We may confuse the finite symbol—the host on the altar, the holy water, the sacred relic, the holy shroud, or even the church herself—with God, and *this is the essence of idolatry.*

It was against this temptation that Luther and Calvin gave expression to the "Protestant Principle," which Paul Tillich sees as the peculiar genius of the Protestant tradition. He has described the essence of Protestantism as the eternal protest against confusing any created thing with God. Neither burning bush nor sacred book nor nation nor church is God. Thus the Protestant principle is a continual warning not to lose sight of the second commandment, and therefore an expression of that warfare against idols that is a part of the great monotheistic traditions of the Bible.

Yet the Protestant Principle has its own peril. Its continuing criticism of holy acts and objects may result in a kind of religious emptiness that loses the sense of God altogether. It may not be an accident that the strange phenomenon of a few decades ago called the "Theology of the Death of God" was mainly a Protestant thing. In other words, whenever we think on the second commandment we should remember anew the first. The positive awareness of the covenant-making God enables us to lay aside the temptation to idols. Or to say it otherwise, one can only safely and sanely desacralize in the presence of God. Otherwise iconoclasm turns into the unappetizing hatred of the world that has sometimes characterized the church.

WHAT THEN IS AN IDOL?

As we have seen, the specific setting of this commandment may well have been the golden calf episode at Sinai. Its larger setting surely was the conflict of Moses with the gods of Egypt and the subsequent struggle with the polytheism of Canaan. But how far can we safely go in generalizing this prohibition? Can it be extended to embrace other, and especially more contemporary, dimensions of life? What qualifies as an idol? Harrelson argues that it is not defensible to substitute items of contemporary life for the concrete idols of the exodus.[4] We can acknowledge his warning and still try to understand how the principle at the heart of this commandment relates to the loyalties of our lives.

My students often express the opinion that the second commandment, along with the fourth, is the most irrelevant to modern living. I recall one particular young man who remarked with a chuckle that it had been years since he had "bowed the knee to Ba'al." But Christian theological opinion has not been so generous in its estimation of human history. Harrelson's warning is made less than convincing by John Calvin's famous reminder that "the human heart is a veritable factory house of idols," so that no sooner does one idol lose its urgency or its usefulness than humankind is ready with its replacement. Why this compulsive commitment on our part to making idols?

The drive to idolatry is a clue to the hunger for unity, value, and purpose in the human heart. In biblical religion, the only adequate source of wholeness and purpose and the only trustworthy giver of value is the covenant God. So the beginning of a healthy existence is in letting God be God. As we have seen, though, humankind has been stubbornly unwilling to do so. Yet the need for God persists and so we create idols. The idol is, in essence, a *substitute* god.

Let us define idolatry as the putting of anything that isn't God in the center of life, where God ought to be. Idolatry is giving infinite significance and importance to the finite. *An idol is anything that is of ultimate concern to a person that isn't God.*

The phrase "ultimate concern" has been popularized by Paul Tillich.[5] It is a phrase that should be understood in contrast to the limited and preliminary concerns that crowd our lives. One's ultimate concern is that which gives life its meaning, that on which we fasten our ultimate values and hopes. Our god is, by definition, the overarching priority of our existence and that upon which the integrity and purpose of our life depend. That is what we worship.

Tillich contends that life must have an ultimate concern if it is to have meaning. A life lived without an ultimate concern is diminished in its humanity. We need ultimate concerns on which to fix our hearts. This is why we create idols. Whatever you love and trust with all your heart is functionally your god. This is what Luther had in mind when he observed that faith creates both god and idol. Thus from the biblical perspective we have three possibilities:

(1) *God as our ultimate concern.* The commandment to love God with the whole heart—the message of the first two commandments—is not destructive of human wholeness, but creative. All too often we have been told that the full allegiance demanded of God requires of us a radical separation from the world. The Hebrew would have found this notion astonishing. The "worldliness" of Old Testament faith reflects the two dimensions of covenant existence. Love of God does not obliterate but enhances love of neighbor and even love of the world. It does so by relieving the world of the unbearable burden of being what it is not: namely, God. When the world itself and the things in the world are relieved of that terrible responsibility, they can resume their true place as wholesome parts of life. It is interesting how often the voices of an anti-worldly religion have quoted the words of Jesus about seeking first God's kingdom, but

have ignored the consequence: "And all these things will be added to you." Letting God be God does not subtract from but adds to the richness of life

(2) *The idol as our ultimate concern.* We have suggested that an idol is a substitute God, made necessary by our refusal to let God be God. Since it stands in the place of God, we look to the idol to give depth and meaning to our life in the world.

An idol is a real god. It is foolish to say, except in rhetoric, that idols are nothing. They are real indeed and they serve real purposes. They can have great psychological and social value. Our idols can become the organizing centers of our being. They can ratify our values and energize our living. Anyone who has witnessed the power of an ideology to motivate a person to creativity or destructiveness has witnessed a power that is close to divine. Given the absence of the one God, who can say that a life centered on an idol is totally without meaning?

We could also add that, in principle, there is nothing in all creation—concrete or abstract—that is incapable of becoming for someone an idol. Therefore Calvin's "factory house" has an unlimited supply of raw materials with which to work.

(3) *The self as ultimate concern.* Behind every idol stands a super-idol that for each person has a familiar face. In the final analysis, all specific idolatries can be seen to be extensions of the ultimate idol, namely, the self. Like Adam and Eve, every idolater prefers to live by his or her own resources and chooses therefore not to let God be God. The essence of idolatry is the worship of the self rather than God: "You shall be as God."

THE COST OF IDOLATRY

But if an idol is not without reality and value and can in fact become a useful focus for life and meaning, why not leave men and women comfortably with their idols? Isn't there always the danger that the iconoclast may destroy the foundations on which people live? There are in point of fact few more unpalatable sights than the angry face of the "image-smasher." Prophets, whether ancient or modern, need to beware of wiping out gods and leaving a mere vacuum. Still, there is a cost to be paid for the privilege of idolatry. Idols have their perils. For example:

(1) *They cannot embrace all of life.* Every idol, because it is a part of the whole and not the whole, is fragmentary and limited. A part of nature cannot substitute for the Lord of nature. It cannot include everything that a life of integrity must include. On the contrary, idolatry exists by *exclusion.* Because one thing or one principle claims to be everything, other things or principles become nothing. If nation is everything, then family and larger human sympathy are deprived of their ultimacy. If a political ideal or ideology is given our total loyalty, then we can maim and destroy in its name those who hold other ideals. Every particular culture or system of values can be a temptation to exclusive idolatry.

This is why idolatry, even in its sophisticated expressions, tends toward fanaticism, and this is why it can generate such power and energy. The narrowing of the field of vision enhances the intensity. The iconoclasm of the Hebrew prophets is mild compared to the iconoclasm of an idol when directed toward other idols. This is also why a true idolatry always has—indeed always must have—its enemies, for any other object, ideal, or value becomes a rival god, a challenge to its ultimacy, and must be destroyed. Thus Rome required its barbarians, communism its capitalist opponent, Western capitalist democracy its red menace, Hitler his "Jewish Conspiracy," revolutionary Iran its "Great Satan," and American Fundamentalism its "secular humanist."

Fanaticism in whatever form is a strong indicator of idolatry, of an attempt to put some false ultimacy in the place of God. Religion itself has often been wonderfully adept at setting up in the name of God ultimates that cannot be criticized but that divide life rather than unifying it. One common form of fanaticism in Christian circles is fanaticism of the Bible. The variety of Biblicism that ignores or denies the human aspects of Scripture, attributing to the writings the ultimacy and perfection of God, elevates a finite part of creation to the level of God. Thus Biblicism can become Bibliolatry. The student who recently informed me that, should the inerrancy of the Bible prove to be untrue, her faith would fail had thereby confessed to an idolatrous trust in something that is not God.

One of the most persistent and intractable temptations to idolatry is religion itself. When a religion becomes the focus of our ultimate loyalty, rather than the God whom it professes, all manner of evil can result. The shabby history of religion, with its crusades, its jihads, its inquisitions, and its self-immolations and terrorist suicide-bombings, bears witness to this sad truth.

The law itself is for the religious mind a temptation to idolatry. What we said in a previous chapter about religious legalism makes it clear that law, understood as a means for coercing the favor of God, functions as a false ultimate. If the heart of idol-worship is self-worship and a refusal to let God be

God, then legalism can be understood as an idol. The fanaticism of Saul of Tarsus for the law, as seen in the book of Acts and described by him in Galatians, is almost a textbook illustration of the narrowing of vision and the loss of human sympathies that is the consequence of idolatry. Hatred, whether that of Saul toward the church or of the church toward the infidel, is a signpost pointing to idolatry.

But there is an even more poignant cost to idolatry:

(2) *Idols fail.* To use a biblical metaphor, idols all have *clay feet.* Despite their real powers to focus life and to give it substance and meaning, they are not God, and at some point or in some area of human need they will fail to measure up. There is little in life so pathetic as a failed idol.

Individuals and societies respond to the collapse of their ultimates in typical ways: An initial response is often a passionate effort to rescue and rehabilitate the failing God or to deny that its feet are beginning to crumble. Often the perception that one's idol is under assault lights the fires of fanaticism. This is the case with many utopian religious groups that begin as socially conscious and aware but, under the challenge or the encroachment of an unbelieving culture, become more and more withdrawn and radicalized. The tragic self-immolations of such groups as the Jim Jones colony in Guyana and the more recent mass suicides in Uganda reveal the tendencies in failing idols.

The death of an idol does not always result in fanatical defense. Human tenacity for meaning more often gives birth to new gods to replace the old. It could be argued that the complexity and richness of modern economic-technological society greatly facilitates the exchange of value systems, ideologies, passions, and loyalties. Faddism is not a new phenomenon, but it is a style of living common today. The word describes an individual or society that can hold itself together only by leaping desperately from one god to another, as a skater might leap from one ice floe to another to escape the breakup of the ice sheet.

We commonly hear today the expression "I am into this" or "I am not into that." One might be into (or not into) kicker dancing, politics, spouse swapping, or even religion. The phrase also suggests the ease with which we move from one enthusiasm to another (today aerobics, tomorrow transcendental meditation or computer hacking) in a flight from tedium and emptiness. The lightness and impermanence of our gods and our readiness to move from one to another whenever "the flavor palls" reminds us that nonultimate ultimates ultimately fail.

IDOLATRY AS POLYTHEISM

The insubstantiality of our commitments reveals a far more devastating consequence of the idol's clay feet. The fragmentary and limited nature of every idol also helps us understand why idolatry tends to multiply gods, to be polytheistic. One's idol may give a sense of ultimate meaning to one aspect of life but not to others. The household gods can bless the hearthstone but not the forum, so we find that when we lack the one God of all creation we need gods for the marketplace and the council, the battlefield and the marriage bed, and so on indefinitely.

We have argued in chapter 2 and in the present chapter that the religious meaning of monotheism is the wholeness of life. Failure to let God be God means the loss of wholeness and the confusion of a "broken center." If we cannot hear the reassuring and stabilizing voice of the one true God, we hear a clamor of rival voices, each bidding for priority. If we listen to the many voices, life tends to fragment and lose its focus. When our many idols fail, the result may be a gloomy equilibrium in which life sinks into aimlessness or despair. Such a life, from the biblical perspective, is not truly human.

Whether or not the loss of the dominance of the Judeo-Christian tradition in the West is the foreshadowing of a new polytheism, and with it a sort of social psychosis, remains to be seen. Some have warned us in recent days that the new "multiculturality" threatens to actualize such a psychosis. Others, more hopeful, have seen the present situation as the overture to a broader, all-embracing religion. This too remains to be seen. But the first two commandments at least reassert the necessity of the vertical dimension for any meaningful human future. As we will see in the next chapter, letting God be God is the key to letting humans be human.

NOTES

[1] Walter Harrelson, *The Ten Commandments and Human Rights* (Philadelphia: Fortress Press, 1980), 56.

[2] Ibid.

[3] Paul Tillich, *Dynamics of Faith* (New York: Harper Torchbooks, Harper and Brothers Publishers, 1957).

[4] Harrelson, *The Ten Commandments and Human Rights*, 73.

[5] Tillich, *Dynamics of Faith*, 1.

Chapter Nine

∾

The Third Commandment
On Using the Name

You shall not take the name of the LORD your God in vain,
for the LORD will not hold him guiltless who takes his name in vain.
(Exodus 20:7)

We will deal more briefly with the third and fourth commandments as they both seem to express and reiterate the truth set forth in the first and second. I shall argue that each, in useful ways, rings the changes on the theme of letting God be God.

The third commandment admonishes the individual not to take the name of God "in vain." Many of the newer translations of the Exodus text—for instance, the NRSV and the NIV—speak of misusing or wrongfully using God's name. I have chosen to retain the older rendering for its rhetorical strength. How are we to understand this commandment and how are we to relate it to the living of our lives?

I remember as a lad being told by a gentle and gracious Sunday school teacher that the commandment meant "You shall not curse!" If indeed this is its essential meaning—to refrain from the employment of the divine name in common and crude conversation—then I am probably more virtuous than many of my readers, for I was raised in a family that did not employ what is commonly called profanity. My father's harshest expressions were "Aw, shoot a mile!" and

"Well, for garden seed!" But my mother would not tolerate from her children even what she called "bywords"—words such as "gosh," "golly," and "shucks"—because she saw them as substitutes for verbal crudities and especially for the name of God. She was undoubtedly correct.

But I did not long preserve the illusion of my pristine purity. While such profanity may not be far removed from the spirit of the third commandment, to limit its application to crude language or even simple profanity would trivialize it sadly. We would do well to recall that the whole book of Exodus centers upon the giving of "the name" and the creation of the covenant community out of that giving. The divine name, when it was given to Moses, was no idle sound, but the creative, active power of the divine personal presence. The proclamation of God's name at the bush was repeated in the giving of the law: "I am Yahweh, your God." So the name of God is not something to be trifled with. It is a name full of numinous intensity because it expresses, and for the Hebrew it contains, the power that sustains creation.

VANITY AS TRIVIALITY

The specific context for the third commandment probably relates to the act of oath taking. We will consider this aspect of it presently. For the moment let us ask about the nature of the vanity we are urged to eschew. The Hebrew word is *lassaw,* which is often rendered as "empty" or "not real." (Some qualms about this rendering will be commented on below.) If this is a fair rendering, then its meaning is well echoed by the common English translation "vain." The Latin root of the English word is *vanus,* (empty) and the English noun form, vanity, echoes the Latin *vanitas* (emptiness). Both words carry this meaning into common use. We may speak of efforts that fail to accomplish their intended result as being "in vain" or empty of consequences. To speak of a person as being vain is to suggest not merely pride, but pride or self-regard out of proportion to the person's true worth or virtue or accomplishments.

Two colloquial or descriptive expressions will make clearer the meaning of vanity. We sometimes refer to a vain person as a "stuffed shirt," and I have heard students refer to certain professors and citizens to some politicians as "wind bags." Both metaphors create the same image of insubstantiality and worthlessness. The "stuffed shirt" and the "wind bag" make an initial impression of substance and bulk, but on closer examination they are revealed to be filled with nothing of worth—with straw and hot air respectively. They turn out to be "empty" after all.

Thus the third commandment could be rendered, "You shall not take God's name trivially or superficially or emptily." Or, to translate the commandment into a maxim—that is, a rule for action—we could say "you shall not live your life without serious reference to God," or "You shall not act, speak, think, as if God did not matter or exist." So this commandment, as in the case of the whole Decalogue, is concerned not merely with action but also with the context or relationship in which that action occurs. It points to the divine-human relationship that alone can make word and action acceptable under the law.

To misuse the name of God is to speak out of a life shaped without serious reference to him. This certainly might include the kind of flippancy, nonchalance, and irreverence that characterizes most profane conversation. It might also embrace some of the religious humor in which we indulge. But it also should be understood to include the kind of practical atheism that marks the lives of even the traditionally religious. Do not most of us live for the most part without reference to God, becoming conscious of his significance only in moments of crisis? Do we not at other times live by our own resources or those provided by society? How many people, on feeling the wheels of their automobiles sliding out of control, have cried out "Oh, my God!" only to return to more worldly thoughts when the rubber gripped the road again? To what extent does the life of the most devout religionist function at the horizontal level and without reference to God? To this life of effective "horizontally," the third commandment reasserts the demand of the first two: "Let God be God! Quit living life as if God didn't matter."

But the commandment is concerned with more than the omission of God from life; it refers directly to the *invoking* or the *employment* of the name. To speak of God or to utter his name can be as dismissive and trivializing as to ignore him. Consider for example, the thoughtless invocation of God in matters themselves of trifling or even morally dubious import. For some people, the name of God comes so easily to the lips that it reveals their own lack of seriousness and depth.

VANITY AS POWER FOR EVIL

Far more serious may be the use of the name—whether with cynical intent or not—to gain advantage or to justify or validate the goals or the actions of a person, a church, or a nation. How thoughtlessly individuals and groups claim God in support of their programs or proposals. The easy identification of God with our own group, its goals, and its value structure, without a sense of the fallibility and sinfulness of every group, is surely a manipulation of the holy name. This is certainly the case when warfare for national advantage is justified as the will of God. This is surely true—indeed, perhaps most true—when the warfare is being waged by those of us most directly descended from Mt. Sinai. The bloody wars of conquest of Canaan under Joshua and the massacre of the innocents of Jericho—can a modern Christian conscience affirm these because they were justified by Yahweh's name? Or can the Christian justify the Crusades or the bloody religious wars of the sixteenth century because they were fought in the name of the cross? While unavoidable circumstances may lead individuals and nations into confrontation and violence to the extent that pacifism may not be in every case a practical option, to use God to bless our human failure is surely to trivialize his name.

There are few areas where the abuse or misuse of God for advantage or power is more commonplace or destructive than in synagogue and church. Such use is frighteningly common among priests, pastors, and other such leaders. It is perhaps most evident when religious power and political power are conjoined, as in overt theocracies such as revolutionary Iran, where every act of the government is sanctified as the intent of God. It is also the case where social and political movements identify their aims with those of God. Such identification is as dubious when it represents the cultural and revolutionary left as the right. There are few spectacles as unsavory as that of a religious controversy in which each side is convinced that God is standing behind it and holding its coat. In either case, to make use of God's name to validate our cause and our truth, despite our finitude, our imperfect vision, and our mixed and impure motives, is to manipulate and misuse it. It is to forget that we are not God and that every human perspective is called into question by his holiness.

The temptation to use God is not by any means always cynical. It is not always easy to distinguish between the moment when we call out to God for his help and succor and that in which we seek to manipulate him for personal success or gain. If we acknowledge that God is God, we naturally and rightly turn to him as the source of all good gifts. All things flow from him. But such humble acceptance of value and meaning from him can easily change into selfish utility. One can wonder whether the superficial "feel good" religions that are popular in American culture today—offering self-esteem and well-being without imparting a rigorous sense of responsibility toward God and the world—represent a trivializing of God. A related phenomenon, sometimes called "the gospel of prosperity," proclaims faith in God as the prerequisite for material success.

The third commandment, though, may involve more than the casual and trivial use of God. It may voice a solemn warning against the active use of the name of God for evil. Harrelson suggests that the word *lassaw* is less concerned with emptiness or insubstantiality than it is with "active power for harm."[1]

This meaning was surely an important one for the Hebrew, for he viewed with great seriousness the act of taking oath. Our popular use of the word "swearing" to mean casual crudity obscures its actual meaning. To swear is to make an oath and with it a serious promise or commitment—that is, to enter into a covenant. To swear in the name of God is a matter of consequence, for by so doing one calls down God as witness and guarantor of the oath. Thus the warning in this commandment is that we recognize the dignity and right of God and not call upon him unworthily.

How might one swear by God unworthily? One might, for instance, make an oath beyond one's power to perform. Or one might make an oath to gain an advantage or forestall a duty to another person. This was the situation that drew Jesus' rebuke to the Pharisee who by oath devoted his property to God, thus escaping from the responsibility to support aged parents (Mark 7:9-13). Or one might swear an oath in God's name to perform that which one should not perform. To so swear is to make God an accomplice to the harm that results. To feel bound to carry out a rash or thoughtless oath or to fulfill an unworthy promise because God has been invoked is to do no honor to God. The classic biblical example is surely Jephtha, who, having sworn a foolish oath to God in return for military victory, put his own virgin daughter to the sword (Judg 11). Similarly, Shylock, in *The Merchant of Venice*, holds up the oath he has taken before God as justification for fulfilling his bloody vengeance on Antonio.

Above all, one is not to invoke the name of God, and thus the power inherent in it, for evil. The Hebrew understood what has been called the "dark side of God." Hebrew faith did not need a satanic figure to explain the explosive and even menacing power at the heart of being. For all of his creative goodness and mercy, God was not one to be toyed with or manipulated by conniving and self-serving mortals. A man or a woman had better not treat lightly the power that can "build up or destroy, create good or bring evil." One should take heed, therefore, never to invoke the holy name to curse another. The name of God is not to be used to do mischief to other human beings.

Religion itself is especially vulnerable to the danger of unleashing foolishly and without due consideration the divine power. The responsibility for sacred office and for holy orders is an awesome thing. The Hebrew worship cultus described in Exodus abundantly reflects this danger, and it was carefully guarded against flippant disregard for the holiness of God. The priests, and especially the high priest, approached the seat of God, the holy of holies, only after the most elaborate precautions and even then half expecting to be consumed by the divine energy. But familiarity with the trappings of the divine has always tempted religious leadership to lose sight of the difference between religion and God. How much sick religion has sprung from misuse of the divine name?

NOTE

[1] Walter Harrelson, *The Ten Commandments and Human Rights* (Philadelphia: Fortress Press, 1980), 73.

Chapter Ten

~

The Fourth Commandment
Confessing Our Humanity

Remember the Sabbath day, and keep it holy. Six days shall
you labor and do all your work. But the seventh is a Sabbath to the
LORD your God; you shall not do any work—you, your son or your
daughter, your male or female slave, your livestock, or the alien resi-
dent within your towns. For in six days the LORD made heaven and
earth, the sea and all that is in them, but rested the seventh day;
therefore the LORD blessed the seventh day and consecrated it.
(Exodus 20:8-11)

The fourth commandment is probably the easiest for the modern believer to dismiss. Is it not best seen as a ceremonial regulation that has stumbled into the Decalogue? In any case, is there any practical or meaningful way to bring it to bear in a modern industrialized world? What is the relationship, if any, to the theme that we have used to interpret the three preceding commandments? How does this commandment urge us to let God be God? I argue that it is perhaps the most practical expression of the theme and that, for ancient Israel, it was the chief institutional expression of the first and second commandments. It built into the lives of the covenant people the correct relation with the covenant maker. It was the recurring reminder that they must turn to him for life and for its meaning.

The language of the commandment suggests that Sabbath observance may have predated the exodus. Israel is instructed to "remember" it. Though this may have been the case, it does not mean that it was borrowed from earlier cultures in the Near East. Most scholars agree that the hallowing of the seventh day and the observance of a seven-day week have no parallel outside of Israel. Additionally, unlike the special seasons in Mesopotamian and Hittite cultures, the Sabbath appears to have no astrological significance, being associated with no lunar or planetary cycles. Harrelson comments, "That is what is so remarkable about the appearance of the Sabbath—the fact that it ignores all normal rhythms."[1] Thus attempts to dismiss the Sabbath as a remnant of ancient polytheism and of recurrent fertility rites are not at all convincing.

RECOGNIZING OUR FINITUDE

Within the Decalogue itself, the fourth commandment is unique. It is the only one that is explained and justified by reference not to God's action in the exodus, but to his action in creation. While the commentary in verses 8 through 11 may not have been part of the original text, it clearly suggests that at an early time the Hebrews saw a direct connection between creator and created, between infinite and finite. The observance of Sabbath was tied to their remembrance that God was God and that they were creatures. Accordingly, we will seek to interpret the fourth commandment by means of the phrase "Recognition of Finitude."

The Sabbath as Rest

The hallowing of the seventh day is predicated upon God's resting on the seventh day of creation. Thus Sabbath remembering is a recognition that life and the world come to us as gift from the working, but also from the resting, God. Rest reflects the character of God as truly as does activity or labor. Therefore it is an integral part of the cosmic order. But the Sabbath is not merely memorial; it is also commanded for the benefit of the human race in its creaturely limitation. Pausing for restoration is recognition that we are men and women and not God. We do not have unlimited strength or resources. "He that keepeth Israel" may slumber not nor sleep, but not we mortals. So we are commanded to cease from our labors that we might reflect upon our humanity and refresh our energies.

None of the other laws of the first table communicate the sense of divine goodness and grace as powerfully as does this one. "He gives his beloved—sleep!" Those who interpret the claim of God in terms of unremitting obligation and striving would do well to consider the bounty of rest. This bounty clearly embraces the whole of creation. The relief given by the Sabbath commandment—respite from the grinding, unmitigated labor that shrivels the soul—is not limited to the patrician but includes manservant and maidservant as well. Thus even the slave is to receive each seven days the bounty of relief from labor, as is the stranger within the gate. Perhaps most surprising of all is the inclusion of the beasts of the household within the benison of rest. The Sabbath is for the beast of burden as well. This fact has implications for our relationship to the natural order.

The causes of the environmental crisis into which we seem to be sinking are complex, but there is little doubt that this critical problem is often fueled by an attitude that could be called a perversion of the biblical doctrine of creation. The Western sense of ownership and sovereign freedom to use the natural order has sometimes been justified by the notion of the "image of God." It has been argued that because we have been given dominion over nature (Gen 1:26-30), the world and every creature in it is available for our use without limitation. However, such a sovereign freedom to use nature without regard to its own worth is scarcely biblical. To ignore the independent worth of nature in God's eyes is to fly in the face of the Decalogue and to forget that our value, like that of the ox, comes to us as gift. So the biblical ideal is not lordship over nature but stewardship. Let *us* be God's stewards, but let *God* be God.

The sanctifying of rest may have another significance, one that is especially important in a society that defines people by their work. "What do you do?" is often the first question asked of a new acquaintance. We tend to assign virtue to labor and to see rest and repose as vice. Generations of children have been taught, "idle hands are the devil's workshop." But profound difficulties are created by a society that defines people by labor and denies them worth without it. Such an outlook can poison all aspects of life apart from vocation. It can give rise to the kind of "workaholic" who neglects family and neighborly responsibilities, finding no value in living apart from the office or the store. It also puts the pale cast of labor on the time spent in rest and despoils it of the healing power for which it was intended.

Like many academics and ministers, I struggle with repose. I find it difficult to retire to the outdoors, as I once did, without feeling a degree of guilt over the work I have left undone. Such a sense of guilt is widespread in our society. It has led us to redefine the nature of leisure time and vacation in terms of labor. We sometimes find that we can enjoy freedom from labor only on the theory that we rest in order to increase our efficiency when we return to the job. Thus rest is never virtuous in and for itself but only as a means to the higher virtue of industry. By sanctifying rest, the fourth commandment gives us the space to be human.

To identify people with their labor has serious consequences for those who must cope with retirement and the resulting loss of identity. If I am what I *do*, then what do I become when I no longer do it? Am I nothing? I recall the pain in the eyes of a gentleman as he responded when I asked, "What do you do?" "Oh," he said, "I'm retired. I don't *do* anything; I just putter!" Even more traumatic than retirement in such a society is joblessness. Often the economic suffering attendant on job loss is less devastating than the loss of "face" and the sense of worthlessness unemployment creates.

The fourth commandment reminds us that rest is not inherently inferior to work. God rested! God commanded man and nature to rest. Harrelson even suggests that, rather than thinking of rest as a cessation from work, we should say that work is a cessation from rest. He observes—rightly, I think—that "the human has meaning in life that is fundamentally beyond the identification of the human being with labor to be performed."[2]

The Sabbath as Worship

In the history of Judaism and of Christianity the association of Sabbath or Sunday observance with rest has been balanced—some would say contradicted—by its association with worship. The connection is not explicit in Exodus 20, nor did Hebrew practice seem to make a direct association between the Sabbath and worship. Many of the elaborate cultic and ceremonial practices of ancient Israel were of daily occurrence or were reserved for high holy times such as Passover or the Day of Atonement. On the other hand, the Sabbath appears to have been held apart from the cultic routine. However, by the time of Jesus it seems to have become a time for worship, centering on the Synagogue; and the Christian community seems to have worshiped on the "first day of the week" virtually from the beginning. This day appears to have been looked on as a Christian equivalent of the Hebrew Sabbath. How did the day of memorial rest become a day of worship?

It is not difficult to see the emergence of a Sabbath worship tradition as a natural development from the fourth commandment. The commandment speaks of the "hallowing" of the Sabbath because it commemorates the creative act of God. Even if, in the beginning, the Sabbath was a family affair, it is easy to understand how within the family something akin to worship would emerge naturally from the sharing of Sabbath rest. The hiatus of the Sabbath provided time for the children to hear about and their elders to reflect upon the creative and redemptive acts of God—in other words to *tell their story.* In time, a family practice would assume traditional and ritual character.

Whatever its historical origins, the practice of Sabbath worship seems to be in keeping with the motif we found central to the fourth commandment. If rest is confession of our finitude and recognition, however tacit, that we are not God, so also is worship. In worship, the synagogue or church turns its eyes on its own humanity, and then upon God as the source of life and hope.

IS THE FOURTH COMMANDMENT OBSOLETE?

The practical problems confronting Sabbath observance, even at the personal level, are many, but they are even more formidable when anyone contemplates a society-wide application. It is surely impractical to bring to a halt the complex and interrelated activities of a modern technological world, even for a few hours. One can only shudder at the prospect. Even more problematic is the absence of any cultural or religious unity in American society on which to rest public policy. Lacking a common religious story to tell and to share, we have increasingly fallen back on our "national story," but even this story is becoming ever less compelling in the multicultural patterns of the present. Lacking a common religious tradition, how can a nation justify or acknowledge the need to accommodate religious observance?

Yet the deep-rooted neuroses of technological society may reinforce the *human,* as opposed to the purely devotional, meaning of the fourth commandment. The growing number of people who have looked for ways to escape from the unrelieved pressure of the business society, the numbers who have sought relief by fleeing from the "rat race," the growing interest in meditation and withdrawal or retreat, suggest that the need for "space" is as essential for truly human existence as are food and shelter. Perhaps Jesus' observation is even more appropriate today than it was when he spoke it: "The Sabbath is made for man!" It may be that one task of the church in the future will be to find novel or alternative ways for providing space for humans to be truly human by rediscovering that God is God.

NOTES

[1] Walter Harrelson, *The Ten Commandments and Human Rights* (Philadelphia: Fortress Press, 1980), 81.

[2] Alfred North Whitehead, *Process and Reality: Corrected Edition* (New York: Free Press, Macmillan Publishing Company, 1978), 341.

Part Three

~

The Horizontal
Commandments

Chapter Eleven

~

"Let Persons Be Persons"

We have employed Luther's phase "Let God be God" to understand the importance of the first four commandments, those that we have called the "vertical commandments." Each of these four reiterates in different respects the first law of covenant, to love God with the whole heart and to acknowledge that all life, value, and promise flow from him. This is the indicative. The imperative message and warning is, therefore, that we give up the hopeless effort to supply these things for ourselves, that we quit trying to be our own gods.

Now we must make our transition and consider the laws of the second table. It is our contention that the transition from the "vertical" to the "horizontal," from the first four to the final six, is utterly natural and psychologically valid. In order to express this transition and to provide a key for interpreting the commandments that follow I suggest a paraphrase of Luther's dictum. If the first four commandments urge us to "let God be God," the last six can be understood as urging us to "let humans be human!" or "Let people be people." If the former "words" have set out the conditions for a healthy existence under God, then the latter words describe the character of a healthy life in the covenant community.

We have already anticipated the relation between these two dimensions of the law. We have already understood that the laws of the first table, in establishing the right relation to God, do not condemn us to bondage. Rather, they are words of liberation. "God" doesn't mean slavery and thus it is not required that we kill God in order to be free. God means freedom! Atheism means slavery—to the crushing burden of being God!

Now we are ready to understand how freedom for God frees up life at the human level. If I must be my own god, I must supply for myself and from my resources my sense of worth and purpose. But like the idols that are my alter egos, I also have clay feet. Beneath my self-assurance, I am haunted by my fragility and vulnerability. Therefore life becomes a continual struggle to reassure myself of significance and to establish control in the face of my finitude. In the absence of God, where else can I turn except to myself? It is, we have been told, a "dog-eat-dog world" out there, with no recourse but to one's self.

Even when I turn to another person for human community, for warmth and fellowship, that other person remains a means to my own end. In this struggle to establish myself I cannot afford the luxury of human concern. I cannot at the deepest level care about the needs of those around me, for in their search for security and worth they are my competitors. In essence, all other people in the world are my rivals—rivals for my space, for my economic resources, for my sense of importance or worth—those things that bulwark me against the loss of security and status. I cannot lose these things lest I come to suspect that after all I am nothing!

Thus my neighbor becomes an obstacle in my struggle to affirm myself in a threatening world. How can I let down my guard if I am to avoid the emptiness at the heart of my own heart? Is it not the case that the "death wish" at the core of all human despair is the longing to escape from the unbearable burden of being god in a world of other "gods"? Being God deprives us of the whole world, even while we seek to embrace it!

Augustine finds the ultimate tragedy of sin in this irony. It is not God who takes away the world; it is "self-as-god." The essence of sin is not hate, but love. When we turn away from loving God we don't cease to love, for love is the essence of both God and humankind. We substitute love of self for love of God. But self-love is self-defeating; it cannot bring the peace that comes from the embrace of God. Thus it becomes *concupiscence,* that insatiable longing that can never be filled, despite its ever-enlarging acquisitions. We pursue the world but, having gained it, we find ourselves unsatisfied. We despair of peace and set out, like Alexander, seeking new worlds to conquer.

"Self-as-god" can never rest, but "God-as-God" gives us back our freedom and peace and, ironically, gives us back our world. "And all these things will be added unto you!" More to the point, it also gives us back our neighbor, because in God we are freed from the compulsion to establish ourselves. Our value comes to us from God; therefore we can relax from our struggle and see the neighbor not as rival but as our fellow in grace and covenant.

The final six commandments describe the character of life in the world when lived with a sense of the overarching grace of God. We said of the Decalogue as a whole that it aims to include every aspect of life. The "horizontal" commandments are likewise inclusive. There is no possible human situation that is not addressed at least in principle by them.

The following outline will provide the framework for an examination of the second table. The reason for the particular structuring will be made clear in the discussion of commandments.

V. The Fifth Commandment: Recognition of Indebtedness

VI. The Sixth Commandment: Respect for the Image of God

VII. The Seventh Commandment: Respect for the Male-Female Relationship

VIII. The Eighth Commandment: Respect for Property as an Extension of Selfhood

IX. The Ninth Commandment: Respect for the Integrity of Society

X. The Tenth Commandment: The Inwardness of the Law

I will suggest that the fifth commandment has a special role as a transition between the first four commandments and the final five and that it provides a means for understanding how love of God is the basis for love of neighbor. Therefore I propose to examine this pivotal commandment in this brief transitional chapter. The final chapter will use the principle provided by the fifth to interpret the last five.

Chapter Twelve

~

The Fifth Commandment

Recognition of Indebtedness

Honor your father and your mother, so that your days may be
long in the land that the LORD your God is giving you.
(Exodus 20:12)

The fifth commandment is not only the first to address the subject of inter-human relationships; it provides a means for understanding how love of God becomes the basis for love of neighbor. In particular, we will see it as setting forth the principle that governs the four brief commandments that follow it. This is why the commandments about killing, adultery, stealing, and bearing false witness are inset in the outline above. We will see them as special applications of that general principle to particular areas of life, perhaps those that are critical for the health or survival of the community and that, if taken in their larger sense, embrace all possible dimensions of such life.

While the second and third commandments in their amplified form carry warnings or admonitions, the fifth is "the first commandment with promise" (Eph 6:2). In fact, it is the only commandment with promise. But why is longevity in the land linked to this particular commandment? Caleb Carmichael connects this promise of longevity in the land to the act of Cain in Genesis 4, wherein he destroyed what God and his parents had brought into being, namely, his brother Abel. To dishonor his parents in this ghastly way was to dishonor God, and most tragically to rupture the fabric of life in community and in the world. Just as letting God be God gives us father and brother and neighbor, so breaking the relation to the one is to lose all others, even including God's created natural world. Carmichael comments:

> Cain's punishment was that as a tiller of the ground he was no longer able to live on the land ("ground" in Hebrew) that God had given him. The totally puzzling reference in the decalogue, that one should honor a father and a mother so that one should live long upon the land . . . that God had given becomes immediately intelligible once we realize that the focus is upon Cain's misdeed.[1]

So the act of Cain could be seen as universalizing the terrible tragedy of human alienation from nature and from each other to which the remaining commandments in various ways speak. To ignore respect for father and mother is to have no respect for God and to make life on the land untenable. Cain became the prototype of human "placelessness" and insecurity for which the only final escape can be either death or God.

Surely it is not necessary to say that the fifth commandment has nothing to do with the abject submission of the child to the parent, and any attempt to use it to justify parental domination or abuse of children is a gross misapplication. Neither does it suggest that the child must approve of or ratify the opinions or the lifestyle of the parents. Indeed, it seems to be addressed not to minor children at all but to adults, and its primary focus may have been the treatment of aging and no longer self-sustaining parents. It may in the first instance refer to the sort of disrespect Jesus rebuked in Mark 7:11-13.

If this is so, the commandment may be directly relevant to a problem in our society brought about by the dual working household and the breakdown of the extended family. I refer to the growing practice of committing aging parents to the care of strangers in nursing and retirement homes. Whatever the practical difficulties that have led to this relatively new social phenomenon, it raises grave questions about the meaning of family and honor. The dehumanizing effect of such commitment is evident to those who have experience with it. Indeed, it appears to have given rise to a generation of "nursing home children" who are determined that they themselves will not undergo such a life, and who say emphatically, "Not for me! Let me die instead." Is it the same as cursing father and mother to show contempt for them in this manner?

ACKNOWLEDGING OUR HERITAGE

I am suggesting that this commandment has a special representative function in that parents themselves stand in a symbolic position in the social structure. They stand in the place of the larger community out of which the child has come. Father and mother are the most immediate point of contact with the rich and largely hidden resources of a person's heritage. They are the mediators of identity because our sense of personhood and worth come to us from our past. They are also the mediators of value, for the child learns within the family the values that undergird the community and give it coherence. Ideally, at least, they are the mediators of responsibility.

If a child is deprived of this mediation or if, for whatever reason, the immediate family fails to communicate the sense of heritage, place, or value, such a child is unlikely to develop the social awareness to which the last five commandments appeal. To honor father and mother is to recognize that everything vital to our full humanity has come to us as a gift. Truly self-made men and women hardly exist. The illusion that we are our own creators is a mark of immaturity. Parents, then, are the reminder that we are part of a covenant of life. To recognize our debt to father and mother is to come to understand our indebtedness to the past and also to the living and extended community they represent: the circle of the immediate family, the extended family, the neighborhood, the village, the nation, and ultimately the world of humankind. In other words, Jesus' comments to the disciples apply here as well: "As we receive freely, so freely we are able to give." The capacity to relate to others creatively and graciously is developed in the experience of receiving from those who have gone before.

We have called the failure to recognize our indebtedness a sign of immaturity. Often the process of maturing involves a studied effort on the part of the young to set aside or repudiate the past. Whether this kind of adolescent rebellion is a necessary stage through which a child must go to establish a sense of individuality we must leave to child development experts. (There is reason to suspect that it is not.) But it is in transcending this kind of childhood egoism that real maturity is achieved.

This point is made in the well-known witticism often attributed to Mark Twain. He is said to have observed that when he was a lad his father was the most ignorant man he knew, but by the time he was grown it was amazing how much the old man had learned. Many of my readers have probably made the same discovery. One of the surest marks of maturity is the "recovery of father and mother" that often takes place when our deepening experience allows us to understand our parents in ways we could not before.

My daughter confessed to me recently with mock horror that she was "turning into Mother," something she had often sworn not to do. Behind her humor was an admission that she, who had never really been a rebel, had reached a point where she could embrace the love and wisdom of that woman with a wholeheartedness that had not been fully possible until she in turn had become a mother.

The recovery of father and mother in the process of growing up carries with it a recovery of community and a deeper internalizing of its worth. Maturity includes the discovery that identity and place and human wholeness are always found within community, and to the extent that the individual possesses them, they are inevitably the gift of others.

The principle that personhood develops most fully and wholly within community and especially in the family community is contradicted by the cult of the individual that has become increasingly to mark our time. Its champions argue that responsibility to others and to the community inhibit the struggle to find one's identity. Thus commitment to family and to others must not be permitted to frustrate the quest for self-realization. Barbara Defoe Whitehead has argued that the one of the forces behind the disintegration of marriage and family in the last half of the twentieth century has been the emergence of a new ethic of responsibility to self and self-realization rather than to family and community.

Seen from the perspective of the fifth commandment, Jesus' account of the prodigal son can be understood as a parable of growing up to community. The prodigal's rebellion carries him into the far country, but his "coming to himself" brings him back into the arms of his father and into the bosom of the family.

Coming to acknowledge our debt to father and mother and even to the larger community that shaped us does not mean an uncritical acceptance or approval. A number of years ago a student came to me to ask about the fifth commandment. "What do you do," she asked, "when your father and mother are not honorable?" The question was asked as she sobbed out an account of family disorder. Her parents were involved in a painful divorce process, each seeking to use the children against the other. Several counseling sessions with this young woman were filled with anger and judgment toward her parents. But one day her mood changed. She had, she told me, made a discovery. She had begun to dwell in her thoughts on the good years prior to the breakdown of the family, and she had finally asked herself the question, "Where did I learn that what my parents were now doing was wrong?" To her own surprise, she answered, "From them!" This discovery and the gratitude it awakened in her helped her play a role of reconciliation in the family.

GRATITUDE AND COMMUNITY

I suggest that the consequence of respect for heritage and recognition of indebtedness is *gratitude* and that gratitude is the dynamic toward the creation of human community. Gratitude has its roots in the past and its efflorescence and outgrowth in a fruitful sense of obligation to others. Gratitude begets self-giving as love begets love. Everything we have said about law, community, and grace undergirds this conclusion. The whole of the law finds meaning in the divine self-giving. The vertical commandments create the horizontal because if at the divine level grace begets grace, so also is this true at the human level. When we acknowledge with gratitude that everything we have has come to us from others, we are able to feel the obligation to others assumed in the commandments that follow.

Thus we can extract the principle that will shape our treatment of the next four commandments: "Respect (or Concern) for Persons." The maxim for action (and for thought as well) that derives from the fifth commandment is this: "Always act, think, feel toward others in such a way as to enhance rather than diminish their selfhood and their humanity." This principle explains our outline for these final commandments, in which commandments six through nine are inset or subsumed under the fifth. As stated above, we will understand these four brief laws as special applications of the principle of concern for persons.

If it is true that the human is born out of the human, and the humanizing of the individual must begin within the family, then the depth of the current social crisis can be understood. Not all of the social ills of our time can be traced to the breakdown of the family. On the contrary, forces within the culture have initiated that breakdown. Lehmann reminds us that the modern pathology of family and community is largely an urban phenomenon.[2] (But one that may become universal as population growth, city sprawl, and the growing reach of communication media threaten to "urbanize" humanity.) Nonetheless, the loss of family structure is closely tied to a loss of a sense of place, function, and value.

Some might question whether such a pathology of the family exists and especially whether there is any relationship between changing patterns of the family and the social ills of our day. Yet even though we may discount some-what the stridency of the current proponents of "family values," it is difficult to dismiss the corrosive impact of current trends upon the family as a value-creating center. We do not know the full consequences of family instability on the fabric of society, but growing evidence suggests its complicity in multiple social problems. The following questions are worth asking:

(1) Given the loss of the family as a structure of authority—not in a repressive sense but as the context for passing down selfhood and for discovering debt and gratitude—what other structure can provide this function? What other communities are available to serve as a basis for the control of unbridled self-interest? If gratitude and loyalty collide with self-interest, can the individual who has not learned them in the setting of the family be able to comprehend or feel the greater loyalties that hold society together? Lacking a sense of loyalty to family, how can a person be expected to have such a sense for community or nation?

(2) Is the breaking down of vocational and gender stereotypes a positive or a negative force in the shaping of the family and of society? Whatever the desir-able consequences that less restrictive gender concepts bring about, is there a danger that the loss of clear-cut "roles" such as were provided in the traditional family will cripple the ability of the individual to shape a purposeful manhood or womanhood?

(3) Is it the tendency of our society to equate self-identity and personal free-dom with freedom from the restrictions of social obligation? This question was briefly raised above in reference to the cult of self-realization. Does such a ten-dency result in aimlessness and the loss of a context for freedom? To what extent is the resurgence of authoritarianism in ethics, politics, and religion a reaction to the discovery that we require tradition in order to have purpose?

(4) What are the special strains that modern industrial, urban, and technolog-ical society place on the family as the primary focus of value and concern for persons? If the family is pivotal for preserving and passing down value, how can it be expected to perform its function or even survive under the multiple stresses of the late twentieth and early twenty-first centuries?

For instance, the significance of parents and family in the shaping of chil-dren has been diminished in recent decades by a number of factors. One of these has certainly been the instability of the marriage relationship as reflected in the high frequency of divorce and desertion. Whatever the forces behind this development, the result has been a rapid growth of the number of one-parent families. We are only gradually coming to terms with the possible long-range consequences of paternal absence. I recall the pathos in the voice of the student who observed to me, not without bitterness, what it had been like to him to be the son of an absent father. "My mother," he said, "tried to be my father, but she couldn't be. I resented my friends who had fathers—even though some of them were not very good fathers—because I always felt that I wasn't half there."

Even when families have remained intact, the ability of parents to shape children has been undermined by multiple changes of economic and technological patterns. The entrance of women into the workforce and the growth of dual-earner families have further diminished parental presence. At the same time, technological advances in transportation and communication have brought children under a wider range of influences, thus further marginalizing the parent's role in shaping children. For example, the great mobility and freedom that characterizes Western culture has reduced the importance of both the immediate and the extended family. Whereas a century or so ago several generations might live in close proximity, this is now no longer the case, so that a child's association with and socialization by the larger fellowship of blood is less likely.

Perhaps nothing has had a greater significance for parental molding of the values and self-understanding of children than the automobile. It has made it possible for young people to escape parental influence and to be shaped increasingly by alternate primary groups. As "peer groups," "culture groups," urban gangs, etc., either dilute or replace the family and as forces weaken or corrupt the family itself as a giver of value, we must be concerned about the result. What cost will the family and through it society ultimately pay for the emergence of television and now the Internet as threats to its role as the giver of meaning?

Is the mindless violence that has become too much a mark of the present the result of a generation that has no heritage, hence no gratitude, hence no feeling for or concern for people, including even themselves? If grace begets grace, what does confusion and rootlessness beget?

NOTES

[1] Caleb Carmichael, *The Origins of Biblical Law: The Decalogue and the Book of Covenant* (Ithaca: Cornell University Press, 1992), 38.

[2] Paul Lehmann, *The Decalogue and a Human Future* (Grand Rapids: Wm. B. Eerdmans Publishing Company, 1995), 159.

Chapter Thirteen

‿

The Sixth Commandment

Respect for Persons as the Image of God

You shall not kill.
(Exodus 20:13)

We now consider four special applications of the principle set forth in the fifth commandment. It seems to be the case that the next four commandments are addressed to fundamental institutions in the Hebrew community. The Decalogue is the law of the community; within its context a healthy people can exist. Accordingly, God's protection and sanctification are extended to "certain matters crucial to the well-being of society." Meyer lists three: "life itself" [the sixth commandment], the marriage bond [the seventh], the possessions which persons may justly call their own [the eighth]."[1] To these three we will add a fourth to which the ninth commandment seems to be addressed: the integrity of society in all its dimensions.

WHAT DOES IT MEAN TO KILL?

How should the sixth commandment be rendered? The simplest translation is the oldest, "You shall not kill," or, to recognize the social and covenant setting in which it is embedded, "You shall not kill your neighbor." It is narrowed even further when translated "You shall not commit murder," as the New Revised Standard Version renders it. This way of translating it is often popular with people who wish to use the commandment to justify certain forms of killing, such as in warfare or in capital punishment. This rendering has the virtue of reflecting actual practice among the Hebrews. Israel never seems to have understood the sixth commandment as applying to all circumstances without exception. It could hardly have meant to the Hebrew "in no case is anyone to be killed." Throughout Israel's history, certain crimes were punishable by death. In addition, warfare was seen as a way of furthering the purposes of the covenant, and therefore it was considered blessed and approved by God. Indeed, Israel's acts of warfare were often understood to be directly commanded by him.

No more difficult moral case confronts the contemporary Christian in dealing with the issue of homicide in the Hebrew tradition than the practice by Israel of the holy war, or *cherem*. In the carrying out of *cherem*—as in the case of Joshua's dealings with the populations of Jericho and Ai and the instance of the ritual destruction of the Amalekites by Samuel and Saul—the killing extended far beyond the carnage of battle. Those of the enemy taken captive, whether men, women, or children, were dedicated to God and, like the sacrifices at the temple altar, slaughtered. The difficulty for modern Christians or Jews in making the Hebrew story our story is made vividly clear by this practice of Israel during its nation-forming centuries.

But the commandment against killing was not without impact in shaping, even in Israel, an "ethos" against the wanton destruction of human life. This ethos was not the only force at work in Israel's eventual abandonment of *cherem*, but its influence cannot be discounted. The sixth commandment clearly provided a new basis for understanding human worth and called in question on that basis all readiness to take human life, by whatever means and under whatever conditions. The degree to which it has saturated Western value systems—indeed, has become almost second nature within them—is reflected in the basic assumptions on which most such societies rest. For instance, the American Declaration of Independence makes the assertion that the right to life, liberty, and the pursuit of happiness is "self-evident"—that is, it does not need to be argued since it rests on the inherent worth of the individual. Many activist groups appeal to this kind of abstract principle—the sacredness of human life. Abortion or capital punishment or assisted suicide are criticized on the grounds that they violate "the sanctity of life."

It needs to be understood that *the Decalogue assumes no such inherent or abstract worth to human life*. In all things, as we have seen, human value flows from the divine *valuer*. We do not have value in and of ourselves, nor does life have such inherent value. God values us and thus we are sanctified. In the gracious covenant act, we learn that we are valued, just as a child's sense of worth is utterly dependent on the arms that embrace and the voice that speaks softly. Our relations to one another are shaped by this truth: our value is not an axiom but a conclusion. We are God's and he cares for us. *Therefore,* we have value.

The elegant image of Genesis 1 becomes the basis for a common humanity and mutual respect. We are God's! We are in made his image! This realization must govern all our relationships to one another. One cannot dismiss as worthless and undeserving of concern that which God himself has endorsed and sanctified.

Thus we propose this paraphrase for the sixth commandment: *concern for persons insofar as they are made in the image of God.* We also propose that we translate this paraphrase into a maxim for action: *We should always think, purpose, act in such a way as to enhance rather than diminish persons.* If this is a valid way of understanding the commandment under discussion, then several things follow:

(1) *Its generality is rooted in the character of God.* This commandment is breathtaking in its sweep and generality. It does not specify circumstances under which personhood is to be respected. Indeed, as Harrelson suggests, "it seems to be so sweeping in its coverage as to lose much of its meaning."[2] But this very generality gives it power and raises it above the level of law to that of principle. Everything that falls short of the perfect actualization of its intent stands under its judgment. This sweeping and universal affirmation of the worth of every person generates the "holy discomfort" that is apt to haunt us—and should haunt us—even in moments where the death or diminishing of another seems unavoidable. Those who have inflicted death where the situation appeared to offer no better alternative—for example, a soldier in battle or a police officer in the defense of a citizen—often carry regret or even guilt as a consequence. A deep feeling for the worth of even the most unworthy reminds us that no "justifiable homicide" is truly justifiable. Even when unavoidable, it remains the ultimate tragedy.

(2) *It embraces far more than the literal act of killing.* We have said that the Decalogue is all-inclusive, embracing every possible act or situation. The present commandment is a case in point. It addresses not only the specific act of killing another but every situation of human diminishment short of killing.

Let us consider the motives that lead to homicide. Why does one person kill another? The specific motives are as varied as those who commit the acts, but would it be far-fetched to suggest that they have one thing in common? In every case, does not the victim stand in the way of the perpetrator as an obstacle or a bar to his or her desires or goals? As my rival, you stand in my path to influence, power, or recognition. Or as a witness to my foolishness, you may be a continuing reminder of my folly and thus one whom I must remove if I am to forget my humiliation and recover my self-regard. Or I may covet what you have—your money, your wife, your land—and it can be mine only if I put you out of the way. At the public level, the use of lethal force is usually justified on similar grounds. Execution is sanctioned to eliminate one who is seen as a threat to the corporate peace or safety. Or it may be required to assuage the longing for revenge or to give those affected "closure." Killing of the enemy in warfare is legitimatized by the threat of the enemy—real or fancied—to national safety, ambition, or policy.

It should be noticed that to speak of another as an obstacle, a threat, or a barrier is to employ language not as it relates to people but to *things.* To violate the spirit of this commandment is to ignore the humanity of my neighbor and to treat him or her as a thing. The ultimate way in which I can "thingify" my neighbor is to kill him, that is, literally to reduce him to a thing—a lifeless body of organic matter. But the ways in which we can reduce or diminish a person or a group of people short of actual homicide are manifold, and they all come under the opprobrium of this commandment.

It is significant how popular usage reflects our instinctive displeasure with being "thingified" in human affairs. We speak with anger of the friend or acquaintance who has, under the pretense of caring, merely "used" us, or we take offense at the belittling or humiliating remark that "puts us down," that is, takes no heed of our worth as persons or reduces us to an inferior level of being.

Thus in the final analysis, anything short of killing that tends toward the belittlement or dehumanization of the neighbor is addressed by this commandment. At the social level, anything that damages or destroys life in community is also called into question.

THE CALLING TO SIN BRAVELY

The chief attraction of legalism in all its forms is that it simplifies that which is never simple. "Rule book" religion and ethics allow men and women to act or refrain from acting in situations that, taken in their full human dimensions, threaten to paralyze the soul. Legalism can become, therefore, a refuge from the guilt that is often attendant on moral decision. Thus to act in a certain way—to be or not be truthful, to kill or not to kill—is from a legalistic perspective always right or wrong without regard to changing circumstances. The simplicity of this commandment invites this interpretation. It says simply, "You shall not kill!

The problem with such an approach is twofold: (1) It may invite us to ignore the human dimension and take refuge in the principle. Accordingly, legal rightness may be achieved at the expense of others. Thus the social debates that often seem least sensitive to the needs of the people involved are those fought over opposing principles. (2) It ignores the complexity of life in community. We rarely if ever enjoy the luxury of facing a moral decision that does not involve multiple principles. What action is appropriate when the protection or preservation of life involves, for example, the telling of a lie? Furthermore, rarely do our decisions involve only a single individual. More often we face the dilemma of affirming or enhancing one person at the expense of others. The multiplicity of human relations makes absolute rules unworkable.

Most absolutist ethics refuse to acknowledge either moral complexity or human concerns. This is part of their appeal. But if we take seriously the concern for persons, we must ask whether extreme or absolutist views provide comfort at the cost of self-deception. An example would be the contrast between pacifism and "realpolitik," (national and political utilitarianism). Another example would be the absolutisms that have torn the political and moral fabric of American society in the last several decades, namely, the doctrinaire "Pro-Life" and equally doctrinaire "Pro-Choice" movements.

Because they sanctify a single attitude and behavior, moral absolutisms are capable of marshaling great emotional commitment and power. But the fact that even within such movements controversy over action and application is commonplace reminds us that we can't easily escape the ambiguity and complexity of human life. It is easy to pontificate in the name of this commandment. "It's simple," said a recent talk-show participant. "If someone kills someone else, he should be killed." But when asked about whether his dictum would require execution of a driver who accidentally caused a death, the participant quickly added, "That's different." It is, of course, different, and as he himself recognized, his simple dictum required modification according to circumstances. The fact that court systems debar killing while allowing for degrees and distinctions of homicide bears witness to the complexity of life in community. Such designations as "first-degree homicide," "second-degree homicide," and "manslaughter" remind us that the question of killing the neighbor is not a simple one.

How then do we keep our sanity, if we have the voice of God saying, "You shall not diminish your neighbor" and we face a situation where every choice threatens one neighbor or another? The more we understand that all people are our neighbors, the greater becomes our dilemma. Which of us has ever faced serious decision without the haunting fear that, however we choose, we will have chosen badly and that we will walk away from the decision with a heavy conscience. Have we not all enhanced one individual at the cost of another? Do we not live with the troubling awareness that, whatever choices we make, we will likely face consequences of which we never dreamed? The "law of unintended consequences," to which we referred earlier, haunts the person who seeks to live worthily toward God and neighbor. In the face of such moral uncertainty, we may be tempted to flee to moral absolutisms to escape the stress. Or we may be plunged into despair. Where do we find the moral courage to act, given our ambivalent motives and our ambiguous world?

The answer, in terms of Israel's story and the Christian story, is to recall the context of grace in which the Decalogue exists. If we remember that the initiative and covenant are God's, we also remember that our inclusion within the covenant is not dependent on our being right. We don't stand before God because we have correctly understood the law and obeyed it; we stand before God because we are called and, more to the point, we are *forgiven!* The doctrine of divine forgiveness, whether couched in the language of Jeremiah or Isaiah or that of Jesus or Paul, is a neglected consequence of the doctrine of covenant grace. Rightly understood, it is a far cry from what was labeled "cheap grace" by Bonhoeffer. Rather than providing an easy escape from the moral struggle, it drives the believer out of the shelter of quietism and non-action into the arena of humankind. Forgiveness is the fountain of moral courage.

Martin Luther told us that we must learn to "sin bravely." Far from encouraging irresponsibility, he called people of faith to acknowledge the ambiguity of decision while also reminding us that we cannot by our choices alienate the loving God. *Therefore we can risk being wrong!* We can struggle to determine what is best in any given situation and then act upon it, knowing that we will fail in some measure but that we will be forgiven and sent forth to new battles on behalf of God and neighbor.

LIFE AND DEATH IN THE WORLD

Most of the persistent moral questions of our day reflect the tension we have been describing: that between the principle of respect for persons and the ambiguity of every concrete situation. The preceding discussion will have brought to the reader's thoughts such issues as warfare, capital punishment, abortion, euthanasia (both active and passive), "assisted suicide," genocide, and many more. What renders such questions so painful is that reasonable and sensitive people who genuinely care about neighbors can see no clear-cut way of right.

Let us consider one such case, that of warfare. The nature of warfare, especially in a nuclear age, may seem to make pacifism an option, while the practical nature of sinful society may make it seem unworkable. Western Christian ethical thought has developed the theory of a "just war." Just war theory has usually argued that war can be morally engaged in only when the goals, means, and methods are carefully controlled and the consequence will be the achievement of more good than evil. But the ease with which the just war theory can be bent to the purposes of aggression and nationalism casts a shadow on any claims made in its name. What nation, bent on aggression, has ever lacked plausible "justifications"? The difficulty at best of weighing goals and foreseeing consequences makes the notion of just war a dubious guide.

Furthermore, does the whole notion of a "just" or "limited" war come under suspicion in the nuclear age? Could there be by any stretch of the moral imagination a just nuclear war? The apparent success of the United States in waging a "limited war" in Iraq should not blind us either to the profound and unlimited suffering that resulted from that conflict or the ever-present danger that any such affair may escalate beyond foreseeable limits into the unthinkable.

What of the moral and human responsibility of the soldier in war? Is his obligation to the neighbor in the opposing bunker wiped out by the needs of the state? Or is it required that soldiers remain moral agents in the heat of battle? Shakespeare's common soldier Williams in *Henry V* gives one of the most telling criticisms of military jingoism and of all illusions about the heroism and nobility of death in battle. He observes, "I am afraid that few men die well that die in a battle, for how can they charitably dispose of anything when blood is their argument."[3]

Perhaps the ultimate tragedy of warfare is losing the sense of the enemy's humanity and, with it, the sense of our own humanity. It is hard to preserve a sense of the image of God or even to remember the unnumbered faceless victims of modern war. Wilfred Owen, perhaps the First World War's greatest poet, and himself a victim of that war, writes of "the pity of war, the pity of war distilled."

A sober look at the other life-and-death issues mentioned above would be equally revealing. Thus the person who turns to the sixth commandment for the comfort of certainty in moral action will find no comfort except that of divine forgiveness. That is the nature of a principle born out of love of God and of neighbor. Perhaps Jesus had in mind the agony of being moral men and women when he promised his disciples, "Not peace, but a sword," in this case meaning the sword of "decision."

NOTES

[1] Lester Meyer, *The Message of Exodus* (Minneapolis: Augsburg Publishing House, 1983), 127.

[2] Walter Harrelson, *The Ten Commandments and Human Rights* (Philadelphia: Fortress Press, 1980), 109.

[3] William Shakespeare, *Henry V* 4:1.

Chapter Fourteen

∾

The Seventh Commandment

*Respect for Persons in the
Male-Female Relationship*

You shall not commit adultery.
(Exodus 20:14)

We are interpreting the four brief commandments (six through nine) as special applications of the principle of respect for persons that we derived from the fifth. The present commandment concerning adultery and marriage has a special intimacy with the fifth because, like the fifth, it addresses the integrity of family as the heart of the community and of the person. As a covenant law and a community law, the Decalogue is concerned with creating a meaningful memory and hope, thus giving moral responsibility a frame of reference. The integrity of the individual and his or her ability to live life with confidence depends to a large degree on the stability of family and society.

It is strange how few people have noticed that this commandment says nothing whatsoever about monogamy. It says merely "no sexual activity outside of marriage." There is no indication as to how many might be included within a marriage—a point that has not been missed by certain groups advocating plural marriage, such as Mormons. It is also clear that the Hebrews as a people did not for many centuries interpret the seventh commandment as mandating monogamy. References to multiple wives are common in

Deuteronomic history, and the royal establishment from David on routinely included harems. What is interesting is that the Hebrews eventually became—and were to remain throughout their modern Judaic history—one of the most rigorously monogamous of peoples.

We have formulated our principle as embracing all forms of male-female relationships, but in the strictest sense, the Hebrew notions of sexual conduct and misconduct were more specific. Many forms of sexual behavior were not considered adulterous and therefore were not seen to be in violation of the law. An example is consorting with prostitutes. It seems likely that fornication was not considered adultery, although under certain circumstances it could be soundly denounced. Since a main concern of the seventh commandment is the preservation of the community, some have read it as "you shall not commit adultery with the wife of your neighbor." This concern for preservation of both family and community is highlighted by the stringent prohibition of incest in Leviticus 18.

SEXUAL CONTROL AND SEXUAL FREEDOM

The detailed regulation of sexual behavior in Leviticus and Deuteronomy reflects the earthiness of the Hebrew character, a fact that is often surprising to more sexually demure societies. Sexual activity was a part of God's created order and thus was frankly acknowledged. This Hebrew earthiness and sexual openness is sometimes held up as a rebuke to the repressiveness that has characterized much of the church's history. Harrelson, for example, claims that anti-sex attitudes "did great mischief within the Christian church."[1]

The accusation is not unfounded, and we must commend efforts to liberate the male-female relationship from the shame and joylessness that has too often shrouded it and, as a consequence, has crippled the marriage bed. Yet it is also important to understand why both religion and society as a whole have been concerned to enclose sexuality within control and regulation. It should be pointed out that it was not the church that introduced such regulation into the biblical story. The specificity of the Levitical sexual rules and the severity of the punishment prescribed for the more egregious forms of misconduct are revealing. They show that the ancient Hebrews fully understood the power of the sexual urge and the personal and social chaos it is capable of creating. Such an understanding is lacking in much of the propagandizing for sexual openness today.

Behind such propaganda is a remarkably shallow understanding of human sexuality, in which the "naturalness" of sex as a biological function is extolled.

It is frequently argued that sexual deviation, including sexual crime, results from the unnatural inhibition of healthy biological urges. Such deviation and crime are often pointed to as proof of the devastation wrought by sexual repression and "Puritanism." It is often maintained that sexual dysfunction would largely vanish if humans were allowed to behave guiltlessly and without restraint after the example of animal species. Such naturalisms are always open to the kind of sexual disillusionment that American society seems to be feeling. Two generations of sexual openness seem not to have relieved sexual dysfunction and distortion but have given rise to new and more perfidious forms. Such developments reveal the remarkable naiveté reflected in such simplistic naturalism.

From the perspective of biblical anthropology, such naiveté ignores the dual nature of humankind as reflected in the image of God metaphor. Because humans are a part of nature, we participate in all the natural instincts and appetites, including sexuality. But humans are never *merely* animals. Their power to transcend the moment, to remember the past, and to hope for—or fear—the future means that in men or women all the animal drives are subject to the anxieties and complexities of freedom. We share with the animals such natural manifestations as appetite. But appetite at the human level, out of fear of famine, becomes gluttony. Insecurity and vulnerability, out of fear of death, become lust for power and wealth. As we shall see later, the wholesome acquisition of identity through property becomes unquenchable greed. And sexuality transcends the limits of biology. Nothing that is a part of our animal nature escapes transformation at the level of human of responsibility and freedom. As we have seen, this complex transcendence of nature is both the power and peril in human life.

Sexuality, then, in humans is never a simple biological function. It has been socialized and thereby entangled with all the complex strands of love and fear, mutuality and antagonism, power and weakness, identity and alienation that are a part of social interaction at every level. To ignore the multiple social aspects of sexuality at the human level is to invite disaster. The current awareness, for example, that a major element (though not the only element) in virtually all cases of sexual abuse and rape is the desire for power is not new to Christian theology.

BUT WHY THE MALE-FEMALE RELATION?

Why, it might be asked, does the Decalogue include a special commandment for this one specific human relationship, the male-female one? There are many other types of relationships in which people find themselves. One might consider the parent-child relationship, the sibling relationship, the employer-employee relationship, the relation of friend to friend or colleague to colleague. If what we have said above is true, each of these would partake of the same temptations to excess and to power. Why not, in the light of Cain and Abel, a special commandment addressing brother and brother? Why the focus upon male and female? Several suggestions could be made:

(1) *The universality of the male-female relationship.* Not everyone is father or mother; not all are employees or siblings, but every human being participates in gender. Even those who suffer the tragedy of biological accident or genetic error live in a world characterized by gender distinctions. As we are coming to realize more fully, our gender identity is far more than reproductive; it characterizes and colors every aspect of our being. Its human inclusiveness may help explain the seventh commandment. It may also alert us to potential difficulties that may arise from thoughtless attempts to obliterate gender distinctions or to insist that they are in every case culturally and socially determined.

(2) *Its potential for human fulfillment or destruction.* We suggested above that at the human level every relationship is rich with human possibilities and perils. But there are reasons why the marriage relationship, and male-female relations in general, are especially so. The key to the "specialness" of the male-female relationship is intimacy.

The child that believes its relationship to its mother is the closest and most intimate possible is mistaken. Secrets and dimensions of intimacy exist between its parents, given a healthy marriage, that they would never share with the child. No relationship can, for that reason, be more affirming or person-creating than that of husband and wife. But it is precisely this intimacy that creates the potential for disaster.

In a civilized society, the normal working relationships between people are facilitated by the rules of conduct we call "manners" or "courtesy." These are the social lubricants that minimize abrasiveness between people so that they can live with one another. A student, let us say, appears at my office door with test paper in hand. She may think to herself, *Ah, there you are, you academic Simon Legree! You must have reveled in a sense of power when you wrote "D" at the top of my paper. You are my nemesis. You are the enemy!* But she says to me, "Could I come in and discuss my paper?" I may think to myself, *Oh no! Not another academic whimperer! She no doubt neglected her studies and she now wants to manipulate from me a grade she doesn't deserve. God deliver me from the likes of her!* But I smile and say to her, "Certainly! Have a seat." And between us and the rules of courtesy we negotiate a solution.

So between teacher and student there exists and must exist a certain "airspace" or insulation that excludes real intimacy. So also between boss and employee and even between friend and friend! This is so for almost all human relationships, even including that of marriage, but the marriage relationship minimizes that insulation in the interest of intimacy, personal enhancement, and trust. This is why the Hebrew did not hesitate to characterize the most profound and ideal relation to God by the word *Yadah*, which, as we have seen, is the word to describe the sexual union of husband and wife.

But there is a profound risk in minimizing the social separation. The removal of airspace increases the possibility of friction and the misuse or abuse of the partner. My friends and students certainly have it in their power to wound or to diminish me, but I am sure that they could not devastate me as easily or as totally as my wife could if she were to choose to do so. Precisely because of the intimacy and mutual reliance that exists between us, the consequence of failure or betrayal is greater. This combination of intimacy and vulnerability is one of the most persuasive arguments for monogamy. The kind of total responsibility for the partner's well-being and the unqualified commitment required to assure trust and confidence argues against any division of the marriage covenant.

It is interesting that, after several generations in which we have sought a foundation for marriage in a sentimentalized romantic love, we are hearing today a new advocacy of commitment as the basis for a stable family existence. Such a commitment can often give to a marriage the kind of staying power that can see it through the short-term crises that often undercut shallow romanticism. Any limitation on or qualification of that commitment represents a division of loyalty.

One of the characters of the television series *M.A.S.H*, when encouraged by friends to engage in a harmless wartime romance despite a wife and family at home, responded with uncommon insight, "I can't divide myself that way." It could be argued that divided marriage means divided loyalty and less than complete commitment to the stability, security, and trust on which the partner's wholeness depends.

(3) *Its family-creating character.* The sexual relationship, whether within marriage or not, has the capacity and likelihood of creating a new and permanent social entity, the family. Friendship does not create family, at least not in the same way. The birth of children makes the dissolution of a sexual partnership a

different matter than the dissolution of a friendship or the termination of employment. Not only are the needs and concerns of new people involved, but also the concerns of society as a whole, which looks to the family to guide children into a meaningful citizenship.

The failure to accept parental responsibility for these new people is likely to have devastating consequences for the larger community. The social chaos of the late twentieth century may remind us of the critical importance of this family-making function. Likewise, the glib reassurances heard in recent decades that divorce has no significant impact on the children of families that undergo it are now giving way to unsettling new evidence to the contrary.

Despite Israel's long history of multiple marriages and the ease with which Hebrew practice allowed husbands to divorce their wives, there is little doubt that in the Old Testament the norm of marriage is monogamy. The language of Genesis 2 sets this ideal forth. The sexual union of husband and wife welds them into a single entity, and any doubt as to the intended permanency of that entity is removed in Jesus' teaching in Matthew 19:4-6.

Nor are the biblical historians slow to point out the frequent complications and disastrous consequences of polygamy, from Abraham to Solomon. Harrelson comments that the history of Israel "implies an understanding of the relation between husband and wife . . . as a relation that is not to be terminated short of death unless the gravest situations require its termination."[2]

In summation, then, why monogamy? Because it is (1) person-building, (2) family-building, and (3) community-building. By contrast, polygamy has been seen, not without cause, as a threat to person, family, and community. The biblical strictures against polygamy are relevant whether they apply to *simultaneous* or to *sequential* polygamy. The former involves marriage to several partners (usually women but rarely men) at the same time. Simultaneous polygamy is practiced today by most Islamic societies and was formerly practiced by American Mormons. Sequential polygamy involves marriage to multiple partners in sequence, or one after another, as is commonly practiced in Western and especially American society through annulment and divorce.

Whether simultaneous or sequential, multiple marriage runs a great risk of dehumanizing the multiple partners, not to mention the children who are the products of such marriages. In most polygamous societies, the plural partners tend to be diminished to the level of property, to be bought, sold, or divorced with little regard to their needs. While we must not be insensitive to the pressures upon marriage in our day and the difficulty of sustaining it in the face of such pressures, it is still the case that whatever weakens the bond of commitment and responsibility is an invitation to use the partner for whatever satisfaction he or she can provide, and to do so without consideration for that partner's human needs. The protest of women against being viewed as "sex objects" is testimony to the dehumanizing effect of sex without commitment.

When sexuality is separated from responsibility in the name of personal freedom, the consequences for individuals, family, and community can be profound. The pressure on young people to engage in sexual activity as an end in itself has resulted in recent decades in the enslavement of thousands of young women in their early teen years to the lifelong task of rearing unwanted children. And the untoward consequences for the children of such children and for society as a whole are only now beginning to be understood.

The affirmation of monogamy and the permanence it implies is a warning, then, against any attitude toward male-female relations that threatens the wholeness of the partners, the integrity of the family, and the coherence and continuity of the community. All of these, as our own society can testify, are put in jeopardy when the lines of personal obligation become blurred. Monogamy as an ideal speaks to the longtime responsibility and mission to build community and tradition, which in turn provides the context of full and free human existence.

What we have said reinforces our earlier conclusion that freedom is not found in sovereign independence but in community. The law is the law of covenant. From the perspective of the Decalogue, one finds freedom and selfhood *in* community. In much popular culture today we are told that a person can actualize himself or herself only by escaping the shackles of family and heritage. Accordingly, one is liberated *from* community and therefore from responsibility.

But this image of freedom in radical independence has an ironic reflection back to the second commandment. The ideal of the solitary ego, sovereign in its freedom and bound by no lasting obligations, is almost a textbook description of idolatry. If the sense of responsibility for the humanity of others develops amid the family, how much of the antisocial and antihuman violence of today's youth can be traced to the disintegration of the monogamous family?

Nothing we have said above minimizes the profound problems for sexuality, marriage, and family in modern society, and all efforts to return to the relative (but often deceptive) simplicity of an agrarian past are likely to fail. For instance, the efforts of some Christian evangelical groups to reestablish the patriarchal family are probably misguided and will prove in large measure fruitless. The question for church and society is how to react in the changed society of our time so as to enhance the stability and humanity of marriage and family.

DOES THE BIBLE GIVE US THE ANSWERS?

It is certain in the present day that marriage, family, and the whole range of gender relations must confront issues and questions not directly addressed in the pages of the Bible. This is why the temptation to deal with such issues by proof-texting is both naive and dangerous. We certainly cannot find definitive answers to complex questions like homosexuality, pedophilia, and pornography by quoting isolated texts from the Old or New Testaments because no such texts exist. But this does not mean that biblical resources are lacking. What was said above about the law as *principle* makes it meaningful even in a changing world. If the seventh commandment is about concern for people in the male-female relationship, and if this principle embraces also the family created by that relation, then help is available for evaluating a host of issues that did not confront earlier generations.

Many questions are being raised by the shifting roles of male and female in modern society. The awakening of women's awareness and the challenge it represents to the traditionally patriarchal patterns of society have required us to think anew about questions of gender identity and human freedom. Such changes have great potential for enriching marriage and family and enhancing all the participants, whether adult or child. They also carry the potential for much harm. For instance, we cannot dismiss in a derisive way the question as to what extent gender roles and gender identity are biologically shaped and to what extent socially taught. The biological distinctions are sometimes designated "sex" and the socially inculcated ones "gender." Some have seen gender identity as a socially transmitted device for subjugation of one sex by the other. Yet a Christian ethicist who is deeply sensitive to women's legitimate concerns has warned against the obscuring of male and female in an "androgynous society." Thus Lehmann reminds us of "a sacredness of difference" as implied in the "image of God."[3]

COMMITMENT WITHOUT MARRIAGE?

If the principle behind monogamy is the protection of the sexual partner (and the fruit of their partnership, their children) through commitment and permanence, then is it possible for that kind of commitment to exist in other sexual arrangements than marriage? It is certain that the formality of marriage is no guarantee of such a creative and committed union. Is it also possible for there to be a true monogamous union without a marriage contract? The answer must be yes because the long history of "common-law" marriages confirms it. But the refusal to formalize a relationship raises questions about the seriousness and completeness of a commitment.

Perhaps no question is more critical today than that of the sexual saturation of all aspects of society. To an ever-increasing degree, sex has become determinative of all relationships. Marriage itself has come to be identified with its sexual component, so that sexual satisfaction is often viewed as the criterion of a relationship. Similarly, sexual dissatisfaction is widely regarded as adequate grounds for its termination.

Many young people cannot imagine any male-female relation that does not include sexual activity. There are few tragedies greater today than the compulsion felt by teens and sub-teens to become sexually active long before physical and emotional maturity has been realized. Thus they become sexually involved before self-discipline has been achieved and before healthy life planning can provide a structure for their sexuality. Our society has the burden of defining the role of sexuality in a time of great confusion. Without reverting to a repressive past, how are we to achieve an open and healthy sexuality without allowing the distortion of society itself?

Other concerns could be similarly examined in the light of the principle of concern for people: prostitution, bestiality, pornography, etc. But regarding each issue, what is clear is that the seventh commandment speaks on behalf of the wholeness of *all people concerned*. Harrelson suggests two questions to be asked in each case: (1) "Is the relationship one in which I find benefit and pleasure at the expense of someone else?" (2) "Does it commend or enhance life or damage or threaten to damage it?"[4] To the extent that either is so, it is wrong and inadmissible.

NOTES

[1] Walter Harrelson, *The Ten Commandments and Human Rights* (Philadelphia: Fortress Press, 1980), 124.

[2] Ibid., 128.

[3] Paul Lehmann, *The Decalogue and a Human Future* (Grand Rapids: Wm. B. Eerdmans Publishing Company, 1995), 118-20.

[4] Harrelson, *The Ten Commandments and Human Rights*, 131.

Chapter Fifteen

The Eighth Commandment

Respect for Property as an Extension of Selfhood

You shall not steal.
(Exodus 20:15)

D oes our principle fail us here? We have been interpreting the "horizontal" commandments up until now under the motto "Respect (or Concern)for Persons." Yet here is a commandment that seems explicitly to deal not with people but with property or things. Through much of Christian history, it has been understood thus: that there are certain divinely mandated relationships of ownership. Especially in the capitalist West, that mandate has often been expressed by the formula of "the sacredness of private property."

It should be said at the beginning that the notion of sacred private property has no roots in the Decalogue or in the whole of Israelite society. It is more accurately a product of the tradition of capitalism. Its author is not Moses but perhaps Adam Smith. This fact has been pointed out often enough by biblical scholars and by Christian theologians. The Hebrew had no notion of "property rights" in the modern sense. The concern of the eighth commandment must be assessed within the context of the covenant community that shapes the whole of the moral law. Properly understood, two principles stand out: for the ancient Hebrew, (1) human rights always take precedence over property rights and (2) community needs and rights take precedence over those of the lonely individual.

Yet, this commandment does seem, after all, to be concerned with *things,* with property, and this is right and proper, because it speaks to a vital area of life not explicitly addressed elsewhere in the commandments. There is indeed a kind of sacredness of things, but it is a derived sacredness. (Even more—as we will suggest below—there is a certain sacredness of nature in and of itself!) But the prohibition of stealing is rooted in the relationship between things and *people.* The inseparable relationship of property to people makes theft or misuse of property a violation of the divine law. Things are sacred not in themselves; they are sacred because of their importance to the lives of people.

Things have a way of becoming extensions of our selfhood. Things define human life in the world; they become a part of a person, and our dealings with them cannot ignore the personal consequences of such dealings. This is true at the most basic level of subsistence. If one man monopolizes the foodstuff available to a community, others starve. Our lives depend upon food and drink and shelter. Our sense of identity is shaped in a physical environment; we grow and we become people by being bound not merely to other people but to the physical realities that give us shape and context. Therefore, irresponsible dealing with place and property exacts a human cost. Two illustrations will make this fact clear.

I smiled at the notice I recently saw posted on a student bulletin board, decorated by a cartoonish drawing in colored markers. The notice read as follows: "Lost, strayed, or stolen: One brown and white teddy-bear. Left ear missing, right eye missing, patch on backside." After the name and telephone number was a notice of a $20.00 reward. I realized that the cash value of a bear in that condition was far short of the figure given, but at the bottom of the poster a simple and adequate explanation was added: the bear had "Sentimental Value!" It now became clear that the dilapidated bear was part of some young person's life, stuffed not merely with cotton but with memories and with love. It was perhaps a souvenir of a fondly remembered family trip or a Christmas gift from a grandfather no longer living. To lose it was to lose a small portion of her life or of her person. The notion of *sentimental value* underlines the connection between personhood and things.

A more poignant example concerned a very elderly couple in my city some years ago. A man posing as a housing inspector convinced them that they must replace their heating system or face condemnation of their home. Then, offering to help them obtain a furnace at a bargain price, he defrauded them of their life savings. The devastation was evident in their faces as the wife confessed, "I guess all we can do now is die!" Perhaps the swindler would have rationalized that "it's only money," but of course that would be a lie. The actions of the thief dealt not merely with dollars but with people.

The eighth commandment recognizes that we live in a *world*, that we are not disembodied spirits. It has been all too easy in Christian history to disparage the physical and especially the economic realm as somehow foreign to the spiritual. The economically distraught have often been piously advised to "take no thought of what you shall eat or drink." But the wholesome worldliness of the Hebrew, of which we have already spoken, stands in opposition to this kind of otherworldliness. The fact is that "people depend for meaningful existence on the material stuff by which they are surrounded."[1]

This dependence on things has its positive side. A secure physical situation is the basis for the development of confidence as a self; it is the basis for trust. This is why every parent struggles to provide a measure of material comfort and safety for the child. It is also the basis for the development of a rich and full humanity. It is not an accident that artistic creativity and imaginative intellectual and social experimentation are greatest in a culture that is economically secure and able to support its people above the barest levels of subsistence. Despite the romantic myth of the starving artist, few great works of the imagination arise from dire economic straits.

The negative consequences of dependence on things are loss of trust, the diminishing of freedom and creativity, and the arresting of full humanity. The loss of trust is felt as vulnerability. The person who has experienced the burglary of a home or the robbery of his or her person may quickly recoup the monetary loss but is likely to suffer from a sense of violation and future vulnerability. So the eighth commandment is rooted in the legitimate demands of human beings for an environment of sustenance and affirmation.

OWNERSHIP VS. STEWARDSHIP

Like the other commandments, this one can be understood only in the setting of covenant and responsibility. Our use of property, whether our own or that of others, should be governed not by right of possession but by responsibility.

The biblical ideal is not ownership but stewardship. In ancient Hebrew society, property, whether real or personal, was not held "in fee simple," but was understood as a gift from God to be used to the blessing of the family and the community. The landholder was not free to do whatever he chose with his property, because the true titleholder was the creator of the land; the human landholder was his steward. The primary recipient of God's good gift was not the individual but the family. The landholder was free to benefit from the fruits of the land and to find in it his own security, but he must never forget the obligation it carried to family and neighbor.

The fact that the land was God's and the community's was emphasized by the elaborate regulations governing its sale. Leviticus 25 details the owner's obligation and limitations. The tendency for property and wealth to accumulate in the hands of a few to the detriment of the whole was controlled by the principle of redemption and Jubilee. A Hebrew could sell his holding, but under certain conditions it was to revert back to the family of his inheritance. For instance, after a "Sabbath of Sabbaths"—that is, after forty-nine years—a year of Jubilee was to be declared, during which year property titles were, at least in theory, to revert back to the original family of inheritance. But the Jubilee inheritance was not a protection for family only; it addressed the interests and needs of the neighbor as well. If, for example, I were to sell my property at an advanced point in the Jubilee cycle, then the one who purchased it would stand to lose its use when it reverted back at Jubilee. Therefore I would have to prorate the cost in view of the fact that his ownership would be of short duration.

How does all this bear on the question of our use of property? On the basis of the foregoing discussion, we are ready to formulate a maxim for action with reference to things: *We should always relate to things, whether our own or those of others, so as to enhance rather than diminish other people.*

PROPERTY AS POWER

Unless we understand the relation of things to power, we are not prepared to understand the lust for property that we call greed. Power in itself is neutral. It can be the means for the greatest good or the greatest evil. The desire for place and for the meeting of the needs of existence and even for the enrichment and freedom physical possessions provide—all of these are affirmed by the eighth commandment. But the biblical outlook denies that we can find release from our sense of vulnerability and insecurity in things alone. This freedom is found only in God and in the supporting fellowship of his people. Failing of that, we find ourselves once more driven to our own resources in our effort to triumph over fear and non-being.

But as we have seen, this is the origin of idolatry and the source of the insatiable longing that the church has called "concupiscence." This word does not speak of sexual desire but of the unflagging urge in the human heart "to drink the sea and to devour the earth" in the futile quest for security. Although the commonly heard claim today that rape and sexual violence are "not about sex but about power" is a serious oversimplification, its truth is that behind the urge to possess is the desperate need to control our world in order to assuage our own sense of powerlessness.

Because it cannot be separated from selfhood, property is never "power neutral." Either it is used as a gift from God and exercised for stewardship or it is used for control of others, and this means ultimately their diminishment. The way in which property lends itself to the exercise of power fully justifies a commandment addressed to things.

The irony is that things used for power and control ultimately turn and exercise control over those who would use them. The dehumanizing power of wealth on those who attain it is an indication of this irony.

Property and the Modern Economic World

The idolatrous power of things and their abstract embodiment in money and wealth was evident enough in the agrarian society of early Israel. It is vastly magnified in the complex worldwide economy of the twenty-first century. In the medieval world, where wealth and power were centered in the hands of a reigning lord, the security of the realm came to depend on the lord. But the power his wealth bestowed carried with it a sense of responsibility in its use. This correlation of wealth, power, and responsibility was expressed by the motto *noblesse oblige*, that is, the obligation of the rich and powerful to display honorable or charitable conduct toward those who were powerless. The power and authority of the nobility, because it was resident in a limited number of individuals, could be identified and even challenged. Although the cost of revolution might be great, the center of power in the monarch or the baronial lord was recognizable and concrete. Therefore it was potentially capable of being engaged or overthrown.

The development today of great suprapersonal and supranational economic structures makes it increasingly difficult to address or to change them. Power and greed tend to become faceless and depersonalized, and economic systems take on a life of their own. As a result, they are no longer subject to any sense of responsibility in the exercise of power. Economic pragmatism without moral responsibility has long been summarized by the maxim that "business is business." This callous motto is a cold ignoring or rejecting of the implication of the fourth commandment. Business is, after all, *people*. The reader may recall Jacob Marley's anguished response to Scrooge's remark that he, Marley, had always been a good man of business. "Mankind was my business! The common welfare was my business!" cried Marley's ghost, a conclusion that echoes the sentiment of the Decalogue and of the eighth commandment.

Recent years have seen the exposure of corporate greed on a scale hardly known before, with the collapse and criminal charging of major business, financial, and economic institutions because of the corrupt practices of executive leadership. Yet such corruption, which has financially devastated thousands of individuals, rarely results in significant numbers of indictments or convictions due to the dispersion of responsibility in industry and commerce.

The Irony of Things and Power

We remarked above that objects are inclined to overwhelm even those who use them and are disinclined to all efforts at control or regulation. This is the irony of things and power and it is the hidden peril in every new technological advance. Each step forward in the control of the material world is likely to increase our dependence on and domination by that world. Since property is power, every new invention offers itself to us as a new occasion to exercise control over our lives. Property, whether at the individual level or at the level of nations, becomes the means of control. The longing for control gives rise to what Marx called the "will to power."

Marx clearly saw the connection between the will to power and property. But his error was that he thought private property was the *cause* of the lust for power, rather than its occasion. So he concluded that the will to power was a disease of a single class, the property class, rather than one of humankind. Thus he believed that the elimination of private property would eliminate the will to power. The subsequent history of Russian communism has shown how little he understood human nature. He failed to understand greed.

Nothing points more clearly to the separation of power from community than the corporate giant that scorns responsibility in the drive to maximize profits. The separation of power from responsibility is exemplified by the willingness of the mass media, for example, to pander to the lowest human instincts while easily dismissing responsibility for the human wreckage that might result. Perhaps even more threatening is the shameless and usually cynical employment of economic power to thwart efforts toward environmental sanity by oil, logging, and other industries dependent on natural resources.

But the most frightening divorce of power from responsibility may be in its infancy in the information explosion made possible by computer and electronics technology. Can it be denied that today a new form of property is being created with almost unlimited economic and human implications? The cliché that knowledge is power takes on a more ominous sound in a time when information—often the most intimate and personal information about the lives of men and women—is exchanged and sold like merchandise.

Even at the personal level, the creation of the "information superhighway" has opened up new worlds to individuals while increasingly isolating them from real human involvement and from the sense or responsibility that life in community engenders. One wonders if the most savvy symbol of the early twenty-first century is the computer hacker, often a young person who sits alone in a darkened room before a monitor, oblivious to the world of real people beyond his walls, living instead in the "virtual reality" of the cathode tube. The hacker often takes pride in his power to influence by the manipulation of data the lives of people and institutions in which he has no personal stake. He is able to do so, for the most part, with immunity from personal consequences. This sense of unlimited power without control is the narcotic of the Internet, a reality that has shown itself increasingly immune from any kind of governmental or societal control.

"A MAN OF SUBSTANCE"

Paul Lehmann contends that there is something wrong with a society in which people are evaluated in terms of their possessions. A man's or a woman's "worth" has increasingly come to mean his or her *economic* worth, and to be a person of "substance" is to be a person of financial substance only. "In traditional societies" Lehmann writes, "the relations between men are more important, more highly valued, than relations between things. This primacy is reversed in the modern type of society."[2] The result is a grotesque reversal of our dictum that things become an extension of people. In our economic society, people become part of the economic calculus. People become extensions of things.

The way in which an economic system can run amok when it loses the human dimension may be evident in the current crisis of the environment. We will comment further below, but this can be said here. If the communist system collapsed because it didn't take into account greed—or in theological terms, because it had an inadequate doctrine of sin—is it worth remembering that triumphant capitalism suffers from the same sickness? Do the seeds of the collapse of modern capitalism lie in the tyranny of its own governing dogma, for instance, that of an endlessly expanding economy? A healthy capitalism requires a continual expansion of consumption and, to sustain it, a constantly expanding population and the continuing depletion of the earth's finite resources.

PROPERTY AND THE ENVIRONMENT

There can be little doubt that the most critical issue to which the biblical doctrine of things addresses itself today is that of the environment. Even those who have sought to belittle the environmental crisis and to label as "tree-hugging fanatics" those who sound alarms are now being forced to acknowledge the growing perils of overpopulation and global warming. The pressure of a burgeoning human population and the harvesting of earth resources necessary to support and sustain it face the entire race with a profound dilemma. It has been argued persuasively that every major problem facing modern society has been caused or exacerbated by overpopulation.

What does the Decalogue have to say that is useful on the crisis of the environment? Does the ancient Hebrew have help for this uniquely modern dilemma? There are those who contend that the biblical attitude toward nature *caused* the problem. Indeed, it has become fashionable in some environmental circles to blame the Judeo-Christian tradition for the ecological crisis. Thirty years ago, Lynn Elder argued that the biblical motif of the image of God, with its notion of "dominion over nature," provided the West with a license for the exploitation of the natural order. Biblical religion was taken to task for its "anthropocentrism," that is, its teaching of humankind's transcendence over nature and for focusing all value in humankind. The world, he argued, as set forth in Genesis existed solely for the enhancement and exploitation of humankind.

Biblical scholars were quick to refute his faulty exegesis and theology. As we have seen, the metaphor of the "image of God" is in fact a warning against the very sort of "hubris" or overweening arrogance he describes. The notion of the unlimited right of dominion and possession is not derived from Genesis or from Exodus but from the philosophers and propagandists for the industrial revolution.

The special status and value of humankind in the universe is not to be denied, either in the Old Testament or in reality. At the very least, humankind has demonstrated its ability to make an impact on nature far out of proportion to its numbers and far exceeding that of all other creatures combined. Such critics as Elder often indulge in the popular mythology that unlike biblical society, primitive societies had a respect for and oneness with the earth that Western men and women lack. But the evidence does not support such an image. American plains Indians habitually drove great herds of bison over cliffs to harvest a dozen carcasses, and it appears now established that much of the southwest desert land came to be by the destructive gathering techniques of early American cultures.

What seems to be the case is that primitive and rustic humanity was still human and was still concerned with wrestling whatever dominion humans could from the world about them. It was not so much humanity's love of the earth that kept their environmental impact within limits as it was their limited numbers and undeveloped technology. It was not the Bible that made possible the despoiling of nature but the industrial revolution.

Once again, the special status of humankind in the biblical scheme points not to domination and control but to responsibility and stewardship. Man may have a place of preeminent value, but he is by no means the only value. The principle of Jubilee reminds him that his ownership of the earth is in fact *trusteeship*. The land could not be sold permanently, for the biblical God insists that the land is his. He values it for its own sake; his valuing goes beyond its usefulness to humankind.

Leviticus declares the worth of the creation *in and for itself* and for God. Thus even Jesus' word that the Sabbath was made for man must be read in a larger context. Leviticus makes clear that the Sabbath was also for God's creation. The practice of allowing land to lie fallow has roots in the Levitical law. The land itself is granted Sabbath for its rest and recuperation against its exhaustion in the service of humankind.

We have seen that human worth is not inherent in humans but is ours because God values us. The same is true of the physical creation. So we can speak of a certain sacredness of things that requires humankind to respect the world, its objects, and creatures for their own sake and not merely for their utility. But as the current environmental crisis is surely teaching us, the earth cannot be thoughtlessly exploited without dire consequences for the people who exploit it.

PROPERTY, FREEDOM, AND RESPONSIBILITY

One issue concerning property is becoming increasingly critical today in the face of growing population and shrinking resources, namely, how do we correlate the rights of ownership and the needs of society? How do we acknowledge the rights of use while restraining gross irresponsibility on the part of the user? Especially in America, where personal freedom has often been equated with the unrestricted use of property, this issue is becoming a divisive one, and a major campaign is being waged on behalf of property owners against environmental and resource regulation. Should a landowner be able to hasten the extinction of whole species by destruction of habitat because he holds title to land involved, or destroy by commercial development the recharge zones of a major watershed on which millions of people depend?

NOTES

[1] Walter Harrelson, *The Ten Commandments and Human Rights* (Philadelphia: Fortress Press, 1980), 141.

[2] Paul Lehmann, *The Decalogue and a Human Future* (Grand Rapids: Wm. B. Eerdmans Publishing Company, 1995), 180f.

Chapter Sixteen

⌒

The Ninth Commandment

Respect for the Integrity of Society

You shall not bear false witness against your neighbor.
(Exodus 20:16)

We now examine the last of the four brief commandments that are special applications of the principle of respect for people. We suggested that the terse prohibitions dealt with above—against killing, committing adultery, and stealing—pointed to critical areas of human existence in community: (1) life itself, (2) sexual and family life, and (3) the economic and material resources for life. The ninth commandment brings to our awareness a dimension of life in community that might otherwise be overlooked. It speaks explicitly to the *social*, in contrast to the merely personal, aspect of morality.

This is not to say that the previous eight principles are indifferent to the social. Everything we have said above makes clear how inseparably the individual and the group are bound together. However, it would be possible to interpret the Decalogue as a guide to private attitudes and personal conduct without considering the public consequences of thought and act. The ninth commandment will not allow us to ignore the wider significance of private morality; it is explicitly public in its focus. As such, it holds each of us responsible for contributing to the whole fabric of community. So we will paraphrase it in this way: it counsels *respect for the integrity of society.* But how does the ninth commandment say this?

The commandment is obviously concerned with the question of dishonesty or truthfulness, but its primary reference is to a particular variety of untruthfulness. The setting of the commandment is the "gate of the city." In the smaller Hebrew towns, public transactions and legal proceedings were carried out in an open paved area or "court" just inside the main town entrance. It was in such a court in Hebron that Abraham negotiated the purchase of a burial ground for his wife Sarah (Gen 23). The prohibition against false witness seems to refer first of all to such court proceedings. In other words, in the narrowest sense, the commandment abjures *perjury,* or false swearing in public proceedings.

It is still the case that perjury is treated by society as a particularly heinous form of untruth. Why is falsehood under oath taken so seriously in most Western nations? Consider that you may stand on the steps of the county courthouse and lie without restraint, and the consequences, except for the loss of face and trust, are apt to be small. But should you enter the courthouse, take your place in the witness box, and *then* bend the truth even minimally, *they will put you in jail!* Why this weighty judgment on public or official dishonesty? Surely it is because when the structures of government authority on which people depend for their security become untrustworthy, then the ability of individuals to trust in themselves or to project wise actions is undercut. If the courts and the agencies of authority that they regulate can no longer be trusted, then a confident life becomes impossible. The consequences of the corruption of the courts are the failure of justice and resulting fear of action and decision. Such fear devastates community. It is precisely this collapse of public integrity that Amos pictures so eloquently in eighth century Israel: "They hate the one who reproves in the gate, they abhor him who speaks the truth. . . . You who afflict the righteous, who take a bribe and push aside the needy in the gate. Therefore the prudent will keep silent in such a time; for it is an evil time" (Amos 5:10-13, NRSV).

While the special circumstances of the ninth commandment concern the legal or public aspects of dishonesty, the broader implications cannot be avoided. This is because any thought or behavior that undermines the health, stability, and trustworthiness of society—whether that of the family or the state—has serious consequences for people. Not only the acts of magistrates undermine the individual's confidence for living.

For instance, what might be the result for a person who must live in an atmosphere of family suspicion and distrust? I recall my schoolyard playmate Victor. I often visited his home after school because he had an elaborate "jungle gym" in his yard, but also because his family amazed and delighted me. His parents were seldom on speaking terms and carried on necessary conversation through their son. "Victor," his mother would say, "tell your father that dinner is ready." His father would respond in kind: "Tell your mother I'll eat it when I'm ready." I later learned from Victor that his mother had a private detective following her husband.

What kind of person is apt to be the product of such a climate of distrust and suspicion? Would such a situation likely breed strong, confident, and self-reliant adults or frightened, insecure ones? And what is the likely effect upon children who live in a society riddled with deception, cant, and distrust? Perhaps current generations more than most are able to answer such a question. The series of national and social developments that have affected American culture since the Vietnam decade have created a crisis of confidence perhaps unparalleled in American history. Some have likened the last few decades to a national loss of innocence. This loss of innocence and the corrosion of the ability to trust are reflected in our language. Out of the stormy sixties was born the notion of a "generation gap," a failure of trust between the elder and the young—that is, between the keepers and transmitters of tradition and value and those who, under better conditions, would be their recipients and heirs.

The national disaster of Watergate caused us to speak of a "credibility gap" between the governed and the governing. The widespread alienation at the polls, the growing cynicism toward politics and government in general, the adversarial role in which the media have sometimes cast themselves vis-à-vis the government, the rampant plague of conspiracy theories, and the rise of anti-government "patriot" and militia groups—all of these give us a glimpse of what happens to a society that can no longer provide a context for confident growth and action.

TRUTH AND INTEGRITY

Our rephrasing of the ninth commandment speaks of *integrity* rather than truth. I suggest that integrity is a fuller concept and a more completely human requirement than mere truthfulness, one that can help us rescue the notion of truth from its simplistic and sometimes dangerous misunderstandings. Many of us were raised on the motto that honesty is the best policy and were taught the maxim "Always tell the truth and chance the consequences." Yet the demands of being human teach us that this notion can be dangerously naive and even destructive. At its worst, it can be a self-serving escape from human responsibility.

One learns, for instance, the difficulty in discerning the truth in the ambiguity of life. It would perhaps be easier to tell the truth if we could ever be sure we knew it. Which of us has not taken a stand on truth, only to learn after the fact how partial and misleading or even false our truth was? We also learn to appreciate our own powers of self-deception and the mixture of motives that prompt us to speak. Some will remember a noted sportscaster who popularized the claim that "he told it like it was." We can well be wary of anyone who makes such a claim.

Is it possible that truth-telling can be made a weapon for inflicting pain or for destroying people? Which of us has not experienced or witnessed such destructive and vindictive use of truth-speaking? Which of us has not witnessed the employment of truth to undermine the sense of worth of an individual or to destroy the fabric of trust that makes for a healthy family or community? Or which of us has not seen the malicious glee in the eye of one who tells true tales to the belittlement or devastation of others? Gossips, after all, often deal in truth. Harrelson is right that "The ninth commandment is directed against the serious destructive perversions of the truth that damage life in community."[1]

The notion of integrity is intended to include the positive intent of the commandment and to stress its larger human meaning. So let us now set forth the maxim for action that derives from the ninth commandment: *We should always think, act, and speak in such a way as to help create an atmosphere of mutual trust among people.* In other words, truthfulness can never be spoken out of indifference to or hostility toward people! Truth-telling can never be merely a question of the facts—even assuming any of us were capable of clearly and fully knowing them. Truth in the final analysis is *truth for persons!*

Given this understanding, is it possible for a situation to arise in which the truth would function as a lie and a lie as the truth? What of the person who takes pride in his or her frankness and devastates people by it? On the other hand, what of the doctor who must struggle with the wisdom of telling his patient "the truth, the whole truth, and nothing but the truth"? What of the person who tells less than the whole truth to spare great pain to someone?

One of the most delightful experiences of my mature years has been that of watching my wife, a woman in whom there is no guile, *learn to lie.* When my aged mother began to suffer from senility, she also fell victim to anxieties. Her chief fear was economic. She could not live on the tiny Social Security check, so it was essential that we help her. But in her pride and her concern for us, she insisted that she must pay her way. We frequently did shopping for her, and every sizeable expenditure caused her great anxiety. I watched one day as my wife delivered to her a medication that had cost $25.00. "How much was it?" Mother demanded. "Oh," my wife replied, "it was $5.00." Was I wrong to smile in amusement but also in approval of her tender instincts? What was the moral significance of her words? How do they relate to integrity and truth?

Can the truth ever serve as the tool of evil? Surely it can if it makes no attempt to reflect on its human consequences. Let's consider the kind of situation faced by people in time of tyranny or war. Suppose a German citizen during the years of World War II observed a Jewish neighbor taking secret refuge in the garret of a building. Then suppose Nazi authorities questioned the citizen concerning the neighbor's whereabouts. Wherein is truth? Should he respond, "I cannot lie! He is in the garret across the street." Or should he respond in some less truthful but more human way?

The raising of such questions, I have discovered, has a disturbing effect on many people. It is not difficult to understand why. The task of speaking and acting becomes immeasurably more difficult when we wrestle with the complications and ambiguities in the process of living. The beauty of a motto like "honesty is the best policy" is its power to relieve us of the responsibility to decide. This again is the attraction of every form of legalism. The notion of "The truth! Always and forever" seems to live in the bright moral sunlight, while "truth for people" may seem to exist in a moral "twilight zone." But it is the case that truth apart from human concern is not merely simple; it is an evasion of the responsibility for each other that is the heart of the law.

The agony of decision that this commandment places upon us forces us to ask again, "How, then, can we live?" In a world where to speak the truth may function as a lie and a wrong choice of words may warp and devastate and destroy, how do we escape a kind of moral paralysis that is worse than being wrong? The answer again has to do with courage, perception, and forgiveness. We act, think, and speak in the ways we perceive most able to create an atmosphere of mutual trust among people. To do so is to recognize our limited perspective and our flawed judgment, but we are able to act and decide because we live before God not by being right but by being forgiven.

NOTE

[1]Walter Harrelson, *The Ten Commandments and Human Rights* (Philadelphia: Fortress Press, 1980), 143.

Chapter Seventeen

⁓

The Tenth Commandment

The Inwardness of the Law

*You shall not covet your neighbor's house; you shall not covet
your neighbor's wife, or his male or female slave, or ox or donkey
or anything that belongs to your neighbor.*
(Exodus 20:1)

In the older Catholic tradition and in Luther, who followed it,
the final commandment was divided into two, thus bringing the
total to eleven. But any attempt to distinguish between the different objects of coveting that are mentioned seems arbitrary or
mechanical. Furthermore, to do so may cause the reader to overlook
the unique function of this final commandment.

It should be remembered that the four preceding "brief" commandments—numbers six through nine—were indented in our
outline to suggest that they were special applications of the principle
of respect for others set forth in commandment five. Note that the
final commandment returns to the margin. This does not mean that
it is not concerned with the neighbor; its language makes clear that
it is. It does mean, however, that the commandment on covetousness has an independent significance that embraces not merely the
"second table" but the Decalogue as a whole. It speaks to the fundamental character of morality as *inwardness*.

The tenth commandment is different in one decisive respect from the other nine. As expressed in Exodus, it has no external form; it has no style of enactment. How would one carry a covetous spirit into action? Why, by violating one of the other nine—that is, by replacing God with a self-serving idol, by stealing or killing or falling into adultery. Thus this commandment has often been seen as adding to the Decalogue the critical dimension of motive and character. It makes clear what the other words leave unclear, that the law is concerned not merely with behavior but with the character that gives rise to it. It makes the reader aware that the "outwardness" of the other nine commandments is only apparent and that they are in fact also concerned with inwardness and character. The words of the tenth commandment and the words of Jesus only make explicit what is implicit in the entire Decalogue.

Walter Harrelson has questioned whether this commandment is so strikingly different from the others.[1] But Jesus apparently saw it so in his remarks in the Sermon on the Mount: "Ye have heard that it was said to the men of old, You shall not kill . . . but I say to you that everyone who is angry with his brother shall be liable to judgment" (Matt 5:21-22). So, apparently, did the Apostle Paul, for he seems to have discovered in the tenth commandment an "internalizing function" that made a shambles of his carefully constructed righteousness of conduct. He wrote, "If it had not been for the law I would have not known sin. I would not have known what it is to covet if the law had not said, 'You shall not covet.' But sin, seizing an opportunity in the commandment, produced in me all kinds of covetousness" (Rom 7:7-8).

The Hebrew term *hamad*, translated "to covet," means to desire or lust after. As such, it seems to relate entirely to the inward attitude that roots in character and finds expression in the outward act. Thus it brings the whole of personal being, the character as well as the conduct, into the realm of law and quickly disposes of any use of the Decalogue as a simple checklist of behavior. We do not stand in opposition to God and neighbor only in what we do but in what we *are*. The outward action is the accomplishment of the inward desire. A good *tree* produces good *fruit*.

The kinds of questions we often hear indicate how difficult it is for many people to assimilate this principle of the oneness of character—that the internal is as critical as the external in defining virtue or sin. It may be asked at what point healthy desire slips over into covetousness? (After all, in the garden the fruit *was* good for food!) And at what point does covetousness become active sin? Can we desire without coveting or covet without sinning? The answer must be no to both questions, because the element of covetousness is inherent in every act. One might as well ask if we can kill without coveting. The point of this principle is that sin is character, and as such it has a unitary quality. Or to put it otherwise, sin and virtue are not quantitative but *qualitative*, not behavioral only but relational. If the relationship to God is healthy, then this health will infuse all our thoughts and acts; if it is otherwise, then the poison of alienation will infect everything we do or say or desire.

The realization that character and not merely action is the criterion of sin and virtue is fatal for all forms of legalism, but especially those that seek to achieve holiness by "self-denial." The lesson Luther learned in the monastery was that there was no self-centeredness and self-absorption quite like that of the flagellant monk. His attempts to banish self by fasting and by the abuse of his body to the point of permanent damage did not diminish but increased his obsession with his own needs. It also makes clear that there is no virtue in inactivity. The paralytic is not holy for refraining from those acts that with strength of body he would do.

Is it no worse, then, to act upon desire than to have it? If this is the case, why not indulge the covetous urge to the fullest? I still smile at the young lady in my class who observed that she could not believe adultery in the head was as bad as adultery in the bed. The Decalogue has made abundantly clear the need for responsible control over the spirit.

There are certainly ways in which the outward act is "worse" than the inward desire. For example, if we consider social consequences, it is often—perhaps predominantly—better to control the urges that drive us. I would much prefer that a disgruntled student be angry with me than to assault me in the dark of night. The consequences for me, and for him as well, would in the latter case be more traumatic. But his "failure to act" does not *in itself* add up to virtue.

This inwardness of sin is a warning against the use of outward codes of conduct to classify human beings, as for example, the convenient separation of people into "criminals" and "law-abiding citizens." The fact that I refrain from the grosser acts of the miscreant is no clear proof that I am morally superior. I may well be cleverer in serving my own self-interests. Perhaps I have learned a degree of social control that he has not and therefore can be selfish more successfully, so as, for example, to avoid spending my years in a prison cell. Or I may have adopted socially endorsed means of exercising the same covetous instincts that he puts into practice through armed robbery or murder. Who is to say that the successful stock trader or the acclaimed politician is more virtuous than the miscreant?

Thus the last commandment has that grasping character of which Paul spoke. It seizes us and will not let us slip into easy legalisms that allow us to evade either our own sinfulness or our utter dependence on grace and forgiveness.

NOTE

[1] Walter Harrelson, *The Ten Commandments and Human Rights* (Philadelphia: Fortress Press, 1980), 151.

Afterword

~

Down from the Mountain

Then Moses turned and went down from the mountain,
carrying the two tablets of the covenant in his hands.
(Exodus 32:15)

Throughout this study, two great themes have been paramount—covenant and law—and I have argued that in biblical faith the two are bound inseparably to one another. However, the relationship is not reciprocal. It is not an accident that in our treatment the covenant comes first. This is both the historical and the theological reality. The meaning of the law, as exemplified and classically expressed in the Decalogue, can become fully explicit only in the context of the covenant. The law is the law of the covenant.

It is time to draw together the main lines of our study. What have we been able to conclude concerning these two central motives of biblical history?

THE COVENANT AS GRACE

We have seen that the story of Israel is saturated with grace, and at heart this is the meaning of covenant. As we have seen, this covenant awareness fuels the deep-rooted hopefulness that in turn drives the whole of Hebrew history. It speaks of the divine initiative that called Israel into being, led her to reinterpret her past, and opened up to her the horizon of the future. Even her sometimes arrogant and prideful attitude toward her divine mission never obscured her sense of awe and gratitude for Yahweh's gracious calling. From this overarching theme of covenant grace, we have sought to draw certain conclusions. We need to bring them into final focus now.

Covenant reveals the unchanging character of God. We have argued that the God of the Bible is not an abstract God frozen in the paralysis of his own perfection. He is a living God who acts in time and enters into dynamic relation with his creation. He is, however, in one sense unchanging: his character as gracious love is constant and invariable. This is the inner meaning of the doctrines of election and providence. It is perhaps the most fundamental insight of covenant faith, because our life in the world rests upon it. As we have seen, covenant tells us that God is the kind of God who makes promises and keeps them.

Covenant builds community. We have sought to show that the distinctive identity of the Hebrew people arose out of Yahweh's calling. This was both the historical truth and the logical consequence. Given the character of God, no other outcome could be expected. The implication is that all true human community has its roots, knowingly or not, in the gracious, community-creating character of God.

Covenant means freedom. This conclusion has at least two meanings. First, since community is by its nature reciprocal, it implies the possibility of responsible and caring interaction with each other. We have argued that any understanding of God or of man that denies true mutuality, and with it real freedom and activity toward God and toward our covenant fellows, is wrong. Biblical religion, built as it is on the notion of covenant community, is not compatible with any form of determinism or fatalism. God calls us to action, decision, and mutual love.

Second, covenant creates community in a positive sense. This is the truth reflected in the two tables of the law. Community with God is the basis of healthy community with each other. Real individual freedom—to act, grow, and achieve a meaningful existence—is not found in splendid isolation but in the reinforcing and sustaining life of love and mutuality. This is true freedom.

Covenant is inherently expansive. We considered above whether we could maintain that the law of the Decalogue was applicable to the world beyond synagogue and church, whether it has general applicability to human society. If the law is an expression of the covenant, and the covenant reveals the gracious character of the creator God, then its universality is established, at least for the believer. Whether the world outside the community of faith can be brought to recognize and acknowledge this university remains to be seen.

Another question is more and more confronting the synagogue and the church and is awakened anew by a serious understanding of creation and covenant. Does the inherent expansiveness of the covenant have something to say about those who are not historically or confessionally a part of the Judeo-Christian heritage? Could the graciousness of the God of covenants prove to be broader and deeper in the last analysis than that of the most gracious of his children?

THE LAW AND THE COMMON LIFE

We are now ready to comment briefly on two questions that are often raised concerning the law of the Decalogue. The first question concerns the temporal range of the law. Is the Mosaic law time-bound, so that it was applicable to Israel during her nation-building epoch but is no longer relevant for the different world of today? All that has been said up to now speaks to this question. If the law reflects in its source the God of creation and if it describes in its functioning the essential character of a healthy community, then it has universal applicability. If it is true, as we have argued, that its underlying principles embrace every conceivable human act or thought, then it transcends and embraces every time and place.

The second question concerns its usefulness in the common life. It has sometimes been urged that the generality of the law renders it less than useful in the complex and ever-changing situation of life in the world. A similar charge has been made concerning the unworkability of the ethic set forth by Jesus in the Sermon on the Mount. Indeed, Jesus' teaching on that other mount seems to go even beyond the Decalogue in its transcendence of the practical life, so much so that it has sometimes been called an "eschatological ethic." This means one intended for the kingdom of God and not for this world.

The Decalogue, it is argued, is a "mountaintop ethic." It is contended that its absolute language—"Thou shalt" and "Thou shalt not"—is unsuited for the foothills of practical experience. Its lack of case-specific law, it is said, offers no help in a world of moral approximation and compromise. It is observed that the practical life of Israel quickly created and depended on the kind of legalisms and coded behavior we have questioned in the previous chapters.

Indeed, isn't the exodus saga itself evidence against the practical applicability of such high ethics of principles? In Exodus 21, the chapter immediately following the giving of the Decalogue, Moses is told to set forth "ordinances" for the governance of the people. These regulations stand in sharp contrast to the ideal image of covenant community we have described above. The first item of business in this "law code" prescribes regulations concerning the ownership and treatment of slaves. It even allows for and regulates the selling of a man's daughter as a slave. So much, one might conclude, for the seventh commandment! And so much for the "concern and respect for persons" that we have argued is the governing theme of the horizontal commandments.

We should remember that this codification probably represents post-exodus interpretations and national history, but the question remains. Did the Decalogue really shape human relations in any significant way, and can it really do so? Is it truly applicable to human life and history?

It was never suggested above that the commandments do not allow for practical application and adaptation to specific situations. On the contrary, they cry out for such and, because they are not case-specific, they allow for it. That is what we meant by insisting that they be considered principles. But as such, they place on every struggle to act responsibly the overarching and guiding framework of love for God and for the neighbor.

It is not difficult to see this influence at work even in the regulations of Exodus 21. The ordinances concerning slavery, though they may seem harsh by modern humanitarian standards, show a studied attempt to mitigate the brutality that characterized chattel slavery among most of the societies of their time. Indeed, they could even be said to compare favorably with laws concerning slave ownership in the American antebellum South.

Indeed, such regulations as these reveal the reality, the "solidity," and the earthiness of the Decalogue, as well as its usefulness in the business of living. Israel was not transformed overnight into an ideal covenant community. The struggle continues and will continue as long as human society endures. But it is one thing to be guided in our actions by cynical self-interest and another to be guided by the principles of love for God and neighbor.

There is a remarkable drama that, in an epic sense, reflects in the person of Moses God's struggle with humankind and humankind's with God. Exodus 32 describes the episode of the golden calf. Yahweh is pictured as breaking the news of this signal betrayal by the people to Moses while he is still on the mountain. Yahweh is described as ready to foreswear his promises to this recalcitrant nation, but Moses becomes the voice of reconciliation. His plea on behalf of Israel is permeated by his own dawning grasp of the Decalogue.

Moses has imbibed the heady wine of community and becomes an intercessor between the people and Yahweh.

Most significant, his appeal to Yahweh not to forsake his people but to forgive their transgression is based on a growing sense of the nature of God himself. He appeals to God's own covenant faithfulness. Moses says to Yahweh,

> Remember Abraham, Isaac and Israel, your servants, how you swore to them by your own self, saying to them, "I will multiply your descendents like the stars of heaven, and all this land that I have promised I will give to your descendants, and they shall inherit it forever." (Exodus 32:13, NRSV)

We are told that "the LORD changed his mind" and went with his people wherever they went. After all, he is the kind of God who makes promises and keeps them.

Questions for Personal Reflection or Group Discussion

INTRODUCTION

1. What would be an example of an explanatory doctrine?

2. If you were to write your memoirs or "tell your story," what event or events would help shape your understanding of who you are and what your life means?

CHAPTER ONE

1. Consider examples in your experience in which a community was created or strengthened by the making of a pact or covenant.

2. Discuss how promise, self-limitation, and confidence interact in human life.

CHAPTER TWO

1. Consider ways in which a person's thinking about or conceiving God might shape that person's ethical view or actions.

2. How might the "religious" meaning of monotheism differ from a merely numerical meaning?

3. Why did the Hebrews think it was important to distinguish God from the world God created?

4. What images or metaphors have been helpful to you in thinking about or understanding God?

CHAPTER THREE

1. We described the Hebrew view of humankind as "strange and paradoxical." What does this mean? In what way might this be true? Is it an accurate description of human nature as you have experienced it?

2. What might the "Image of God" metaphor in Genesis 2 tell us about our human nature? In what way is being in God's image a blessing? In what way is it a burden or curse?

3. Think about the different bonds that constitute the communities of which you are a part. In what ways are they positive and inclusive? How are they exclusive? Have you ever been hurt by exclusion?

4. Do you tend to think of time as cyclical or linear? What has influenced your thinking?

CHAPTER FOUR

1. Consider the two types of religion described on pages 45 and 46. Into which type do you most easily fit? Are you always consistent?

2. Legalism is referred to as "the nursery floor of religion." What might this metaphor mean?

3. How might a call to covenant require that we take human freedom seriously?

CHAPTER FIVE

1. We have referred to the "negative form" of the commandments as a "freer of space." What might this notion mean?

2. We have argued that the brevity and generality of the commandments free them from time and place. In what ways might this be true?

3. Think about what we called the "di-unity" of the commandments. How might the two "tables" of the law require and reinforce one another?

4. Do Christians still struggle over the question of particularism and universality? In what ways?

CHAPTER SIX

1. How does the brief preface to the Ten Commandments give them meaning?

2. In what ways is the preface a demand? In what ways an affirmation?

CHAPTER SEVEN

1. What might it mean to refer to Moses as a "practical monotheist"?

2. Discuss the difference between an abstract oneness and an "organic" oneness. How can a living thing (either God or a finite thing) be a dynamic, changing being and yet be viewed as one?

3. What do you believe Karl Barth meant by the divine "Yes" hidden behind the divine "No"?

CHAPTER EIGHT

1. Consider some of the biblical metaphors we use to describe God—for instance, "Father," "Light of the World," "Rock of Ages." In what ways might they enrich our understanding of God? Might they promote misunderstandings?

2. Discuss the virtues and the dangers in what we referred to as the "Catholic substance" and the "Protestant Principle."

3. Consider the definition of an idol in italics on page 106. Employing this definition, what do you believe are the most prevalent forms of idolatry today?

4. What might Calvin have meant when he spoke of the human heart as the "factory house" of idols?

CHAPTER NINE

1. Can you think of examples in our day of individuals, institutions or other organizations, or nations using the name of God for evil?

CHAPTER TEN

1. We referred to the fourth commandment as "the most practical expression" of the principle of letting God be God. In what way or ways might this be so?

2. What problems might a complex technological society pose for observing or honoring the fourth commandment? How might we honor its deepest intentions in such a world?

CHAPTER TWELVE

1. In what way might the fifth commandment provide a bridge between the first four and the final five?

2. Discuss the proposition that "the human is born out of the human."

3. Is the breakdown of the family in our society unique in degree? What are some of the symptoms of such a breakdown? Does the fifth commandment offer help in coping with the problem?

4. What are the most serious threats in our day to family and community?

CHAPTER THIRTEEN

1. In what ways other than killing does society diminish people? In what ways can the individual diminish others?

2. "Just war theory" has been employed in recent days by government spokes-people to defend military initiatives. Is such a theory allowed by the sixth commandment, especially in a nuclear age? Why? Why not?

CHAPTER FOURTEEN

1. What are we to make of the so-called "sexual revolution" of our century? In what ways has it enriched the relation of male and female? In what ways has it opened the way to human and family diminishment?

2. In view of the sexual saturation of modern society, what can be done to preserve the relation between sexuality and responsibility?

CHAPTER FIFTEEN

1. If "the sacredness of private property" is not sanctioned by the command-ments or by the Bible, how does this bear on business ethics? Is unrestricted capitalism justifiable under the eighth commandment?

2. What limits on free acquisition could be justified?

3. Consider the relationship between the will to own and the will to control.

4. In what way might the eighth commandment provide the basis for a "healthy materialism"? What would constitute a healthy materialism? How would it differ from other less healthy kinds?

5. What resources do Hebrew faith in general and the commandments in par-ticular provide for better understanding and coping with the environmental crisis of our time?

CHAPTER SIXTEEN

1. Is the distinction between truth telling and integrity a valid one? Is it useful?

2. What are the chief threats to building a society in which mutual trust is possible? Consider, for example, air and water pollution, urban violence, the merchandizing of personal data, loss of privacy, identity theft, terrorism, etc.

CHAPTER SEVENTEEN

1. The tenth commandment makes clear the concern of the law with character as well as conduct. Should intent be a consideration in the action of a jury in a court?

2. Is "adultery in the head" as serious a matter as "adultery in the bed"? How does the tenth commandment help us understand the nature of sin?